Women in Britain

WESTON
COLLEGE
LIBRARY

London: H M S O

Researched and written by Publishing Services, Central Office of Information.

ISBN 0 11 701982 8

HMSO

HMSO publications are available from:

HMSO Publications Centre
(Mail, fax and telephone orders only)
PO Box 276, London SW8 5DT
Telephone orders 0171 873 9090
General enquiries 0171 873 0011
(queuing system in operation for both numbers)
Fax orders 0171 873 8200

HMSO Bookshops
49 High Holborn, London WC1V 6HB
(counter service only)
0171 873 0011   Fax 0171 831 1326
68–69 Bull Street, Birmingham B4 6AD
0121 236 9696 Fax 0121 236 9699
33 Wine Street, Bristol BS1 2BQ
0117 9264306   Fax 0117 9294515
9–21 Princess Street, Manchester M60 8AS
0161 834 7201   Fax 0161 833 0634
16 Arthur Street, Belfast BT1 4GD
01232 238451   Fax 01232 235401
71 Lothian Road, Edinburgh EH3 9AZ
0131 228 4181   Fax 0131 229 2734
The HMSO Oriel Bookshop
The Friary, Cardiff CF1 4AA
01222 395548   Fax 01222 384347

HMSO's Accredited Agents
(see Yellow Pages)

and through good booksellers

Contents

Acknowledgments

The Central Office of Information would like to thank the following organisations for their co-operation in compiling this book: the Department for Education and Employment, the Cabinet Office, The Scottish Office, the Welsh Office, the Northern Ireland Office, the Equal Opportunities Commission, the Home Office, the Department of Health, the Department of National Heritage, the Department of Social Security, the Department of Transport, the Ministry of Defence and the Sports Council.

Cover Photograph Credit

Format.

Introduction

The role and status of women in Britain[1] have changed substantially in recent decades. Women today play a more active role in areas of public life such as politics, business, education, the media and sport, and there are growing numbers of women appointed on public bodies. As in other industrialised countries, more women are in work than ever before, with Britain having the third highest proportion of women in work in the European Union (EU). Growing numbers of women are combining work and raising a family and more women are returning to work after having children.

Women outnumber men—in mid-1994 the population comprised 29.8 million females and 28.6 million males. There are fewer female births though and in the younger age groups there are more males than females. Male mortality is higher at all ages, so that beyond the age of 50 the number of women exceeds the number of men and beyond 60 women significantly outnumber men.[2]

Important progress towards equality of opportunity has been achieved in the past 25 years through legislation in areas such as employment, education, personal taxation and social welfare. Inequalities of opportunity and under-achievement remain though. For example:

[1] The term 'Britain' is used in this book to mean the United Kingdom of Great Britain and Northern Ireland; 'Great Britain' comprises England, Scotland and Wales.
[2] Detailed statistics on population and many other subjects are included in *Social Focus on Women* compiled by the Central Statistical Office and issued in August 1995 (see Further Reading).

—women are under-represented in Parliament and in other positions in public life;

—there are relatively few women at senior levels in business and the professions;

—women tend to bear much of the responsibility for caring for children and for elderly, sick and disabled relatives; and

—a disproportionately large number of women workers are in lower paid, lower status jobs.

In responding to these and other problems, the Government's policy is to implement fully and, where necessary, build upon legislation which provides women with a firm basis for pursuing equality of opportunity. It also seeks to initiate and support practical measures aimed at widening opportunities for women in education, training and employment; and to create the economic prosperity to provide more job opportunities for both men and women. While encouraging women to follow careers in areas traditionally occupied by men, the Government recognises the equally valuable role played by housewives, mothers and voluntary carers for sick and elderly people.

This book describes the contribution made by women to national life, the role played by government departments and agencies concerned with sex equality, and legislation relating to the position of women in society. Progress towards greater equality is outlined in areas such as education, employment, social welfare and criminal justice. This book also outlines Britain's involvement in international co-operation. Britain is committed to the aims of the United Nations (UN) policy concerning women and participated fully in the fourth UN World Conference on Women held in Peking in September 1995.

Historical Perspective

At the beginning of the 19th century, women had relatively few opportunities. The Industrial Revolution and associated changes had eliminated many of their traditional work and domestic activities. Almost the only paid occupations open to educated women of limited means were those of governess or 'companion'. The main employment for less-educated women was domestic service. Women drawn into the new textile mills, factories and workshops usually worked in the least-skilled and lowest-paid jobs. Women also had fewer rights—for example, they did not have the right to vote, and married women were not allowed to hold property.

During the 19th and 20th centuries major changes in legal status have been made by Parliament and practically all positive legal discrimination based on gender has been removed. Fundamental improvements in women's lives have also resulted from changes in social attitudes, demographic changes and a revolution in the pattern of family and social life.

Women Pioneers

During the 19th century the change in women's status resulted in part from the work of exceptional women. There were, for example, novelists such as Jane Austen, the Brontë sisters, George Eliot and Elizabeth Gaskell; the poet Elizabeth Barrett Browning; and women such as Mary Wollstonecraft and Mrs Henry Reid who wrote on the rights of women. Humanitarians included Elizabeth Fry, pioneer of prison reform; Mary Carpenter, the champion of vagrant, neglected or delinquent children; Josephine Butler, who helped unmarried mothers and prostitutes; and Louise Twining, who campaigned for better treatment of old people in workhouses.

Other women fought for better industrial conditions for their sex: Emma Paterson founded the Women's Trade Union League in 1874, in the period before women were admitted to the established trade unions on the same basis as men; and Beatrice Webb played a large part in the establishment of Trade Boards to regulate wages and conditions in the unorganised industries in which many women were employed.

Educationists included Frances Mary Buss, headmistress of the North London Collegiate School (founded 1850); Dorothea Beale, headmistress of Cheltenham Ladies' College (founded 1853); Emily Davies, whose efforts resulted in the founding of Girton College, Cambridge in 1860; and Anne Clough, first principal of Newnham College, Cambridge (founded 1875). The first women doctors included Elizabeth Blackwell, who was obliged to qualify in the United States, and Elizabeth Garrett Anderson and Sophia Jex Blake, who carried on the struggle to gain admission for women to the medical profession, which was finally granted in 1876. Florence Nightingale was the founder of modern nursing.

Structural Changes

Women gradually began to work in areas previously exclusive to men—in military hospitals overseas and in the larger retail shops. The invention of the telephone and the typewriter provided more occupations for women. The Civil Service began to employ women typists in 1888 and by the end of the 19th century women were working in commercial offices in increasing numbers.

Table 1: Women at Work and in Public Life: Some Important 'Firsts'

1919	Woman Member of Parliament to take a seat in the House of Commons, Nancy Astor.
1929	Cabinet minister, Margaret Bondfield.
1943	President of the Trades Union Congress, Anne Loughlin.
1945	Prison governor, Charity Taylor.
1948	University vice-chancellor, Professor Lillian Penson.
1949	King's Counsel (Senior Barrister), Rose Heilbron and Helena Normanton.
1955	Head of Civil Service Department (Permanent Secretary), Evelyn Sharp.
1958	Life Peeress, Baroness Wootton of Abinger.
	Bank manager, Hilda Harding.
1964	British Nobel Prizewinner (for chemistry), Dorothy Hodgkin.
1965	High Court judge, Elizabeth Lane.
1973	British High Commissioner, Eleanor Emery.
	Director of a national museum (the Science Museum), Margaret Weston.
1974	Captain of the Gentleman-at-Arms (Government Chief Whip, House of Lords), Lady Llewelyn Davies.
1975	Leader of the official Opposition, Margaret Thatcher.
1976	British Ambassador, Anne Warburton.
1979	Prime Minister, Margaret Thatcher.
1981	Leader of the House of Lords, Baroness Young.
1983	Lord Mayor of London, Dame Mary Donaldson.
1984	Law Commissioner, Brenda Hoggett.
	Trade union general secretary, Brenda Dean.
1987	Court of Appeal Judge, Dame Elizabeth Butler-Sloss.
1991	British woman in space, Helen Sharman.
1992	Speaker of the House of Commons, Betty Boothroyd.
1993	British woman to climb Everest, Rebecca Stephens.
1994	Priest ordained in the Church of England, Angela Berners-Wilson.
1995	Chief constable, Pauline Clare.

The First World War gave women much wider opportunities to exercise their abilities. Gaps left by men who joined the armed forces were filled by women. The number of women at work rose by nearly a quarter. The greatest number were employed in industry, and out of half a million who entered the metal trades, some 90 per cent were engaged in work normally done by men. Women were also employed in public transport and in other public services, in professional and semi-professional occupations, in the police and in the Women's Land Army. In the Civil Service between 1914 and 1919 the number of women rose from 600 to nearly 170,000. The women's auxiliary services were formed in conjunction with the Royal Navy, the Army and the Royal Air Force, bringing women for the first time into the military organisation of war.

Women's contribution to the war effort brought about a change in public opinion. The right of entry to most professions was formally granted to women by the Sex Disqualification (Removal) Act 1919. Subsequently, it became increasingly accepted that girls should be properly educated and trained for employment. Large numbers of educated women were already working in nursing, teaching and secretarial jobs, and more began to enter the old-established professions or the newer professions such as advertising and broadcasting which developed in the 1920s and 1930s.

Parliamentary Representation

Various electoral reform measures were introduced in the 19th century, so that by the mid-1880s most adult males had the right to vote. Demand for the right of women to vote grew. The first regular suffrage committee was set up in 1855. From the 1860s until the outbreak of the First World War in 1914, groups of women—led by Millicent Fawcett and her colleagues as well as by 'militant' suffragettes such as Emmeline Pankhurst and her daughter Christabel—worked steadily for the enfranchisement of women. This was eventually achieved in two Acts in 1918 (see Table 2), which granted women over the age of 30 the right to vote and the right for women to be elected to the House of Commons. In 1928 the minimum voting age for women was lowered to 21, the same as for men.

An Act of 1907 had confirmed the right of women to be elected as county or borough councillors and in 1908 a woman mayor was appointed for the first time. Since 1919, when Lady Astor took her seat, there have always been women in the House of Commons. The first to become a government minister was Margaret Bondfield, Minister of Labour (and a member of the Cabinet) in 1929.

Social and Family Changes

After 1920 the structure of British social and family life began to change radically, with the spread of knowledge of contraceptive methods, the associated fall in the birth rate and the development of health and social services and of labour-saving devices in the home. During the Second World War, women again replaced men called up to serve in the armed forces, and thus undertook heavy, skilled or specialised jobs normally done by men. Women also served in the armed forces.

Some of the immediate impact of the Second World War on the position of women was lost with the return of peacetime conditions. However, social and family changes have continued. Among the most significant are:

—a decline in the number of marriages;

—more marriages ending in divorce, including second and subsequent marriages;

—an increase in cohabitation, both before marriage and as longer-term relationships;

—growth in the number of lone parents;

—a big increase in births outside marriage;

—more people living alone;

—a decline in the number of large families; and

—greater life expectancy, with a growing number of old people, especially the very elderly.

Recent Developments

Since 1970 Parliament has enacted major legislation to promote equality of opportunity and to eliminate discrimination in many other fields including employment and education. Three important Acts passed were the Equal Pay Act 1970 and the Sex Discrimination Acts of 1975 and 1986.

Women have become more prominent in many areas of public life. The first woman to be elected as the leader of a major political party was Margaret Thatcher, who became leader of the Conservative Party in 1975 and Britain's first woman Prime Minister in 1979. In 1992 the Church of England voted for the ordination of women priests, and in March 1994 the first 32 priests were ordained in a service at Bristol Cathedral. Other examples are given in the following sections.

Table 2: Important Advances for Women's Rights

1869	Women ratepayers get the vote in local elections.
1907	Women win right to be elected as county or borough councillors.
1918	Women over 30 get the right to vote in general elections: Representation of the People Act.
	Women win right to be elected as members of the House of Commons: Parliament (Qualification of Women) Act.
1919	Right of entry to most professions formally granted to women: Sex Disqualification (Removal) Act.
1928	All women over 21 get the vote: Representation of the People (Equal Franchise) Act.
1945	Family allowances paid direct to mothers.
1969	Wives can enter into financial and legal contracts in their own right.
1970	Right to equal treatment where men and women do the same or broadly similar work: Equal Pay Act.
1973	Equal rights of guardianship of children.
1975	Sex discrimination unlawful in employment, training, education, and the provision of housing, services, goods and facilities to the public: Sex Discrimination Act.
	Right to paid maternity leave and other rights for working women: Employment Protection Act.
1980	Equality of entitlement to most social security benefits.
1983	Equal pay for women for work of equal value: Equal Pay (Amendment) Regulations.
1986	Equal retirement ages for men and women: Sex Discrimination Act.
1988	Independent taxation for husband and wife: Finance Act.
1993	Dismissal of a pregnant worker because of her pregnancy made automatically unfair, and maternity rights extended and enhanced: Trade Union Reform and Employment Rights Act.
1995	Arrangements for future equalisation of state pension age and equal treatment for occupational pensions: Pensions Act.

Note: In some cases the legislation took effect at a later date. For example, the Equal Pay Act 1970 came into force in 1975 and the system of independent taxation for husband and wife was implemented in 1990.

Participation in Public Life

Women enjoy the same political rights as men, and may vote in parliamentary and local elections, be elected to the House of Commons or to local councils and sit in the House of Lords. Britain has acceded to the 1952 United Nations Convention on the Political Rights of Women.

Politics

There has been an increase in the number of women Members of Parliament (MPs) in recent general elections (see Table 3). In October 1995 there were 63 women MPs, accounting for 9.7 per cent of MPs: 38 Labour MPs, 18 Conservative, 3 Liberal Democrat, 2 Scottish National Party, the Speaker and one of the Deputy Speakers. Women form a smaller proportion—around 6 per cent—of the members of the House of Lords. Most are life peeresses, as few hereditary titles are held by women, and women account for 14 per cent of the total of life peers and peeresses. On the other hand there are relatively more women members of the European Parliament (MEPs). In the 1994 election 16 of the 87 MEPs elected for constituencies in Britain were women: 18 per cent, compared with 15 per cent in the 1984 election.

In 1979 the then Prime Minister, Margaret Thatcher, became the first woman in either Western Europe or North America to rise to the highest national political office. She was Prime Minister for over 11 years until November 1990, the longest-serving holder of the office in the 20th century.

Table 3: Women MPs elected in General Elections

	Number of women MPs	% of MPs
1983	23	*3.5*
1987	41	*6.3*
1992	60	*9.2*

Source: House of Commons Public Information Office.

Note: Following by-elections since 1992, the number of women MPs has increased to 63.

In October 1995 there were nine women government ministers. Two serve in the Cabinet: Virginia Bottomley as Secretary of State for National Heritage and Gillian Shephard as Secretary of State for Education and Employment. Four are ministers of state: Ann Widdecombe and Baroness Blatch (both at the Home Office), Angela Knight (Economic Secretary, HM Treasury), and Baroness Chalker (Minister for Overseas Development).

Women also hold senior positions in the other main political parties. Margaret Beckett, then deputy leader of the Labour Party, became acting leader following the death of the party leader John Smith in May 1994 and held this post until the new leader was elected in July 1994; she is now spokesman on trade and industry. Five other women are in the Shadow Cabinet: Harriet Harman (health), Marjorie Mowlam (Northern Ireland), Joan Lestor (overseas development), Clare Short (transport) and Ann Taylor (shadow Leader of the House). Other Labour Party spokesmen include Tessa Jowell on women's issues, Joan Ruddock (environmental protection) and Llin Golding (food and drink industries). Pauline Green is the first British president of the Parliamentary

Group of European Socialists in the European Parliament, having previously been leader of the European Parliamentary Labour Party. The three women Liberal Democrat MPs are all spokesmen: Ray Michie (deputy convenor on Scotland), Liz Lynne (social security and disability) and Diana Maddock (family and women's issues, and housing).

Betty Boothroyd became the first woman Speaker of the House of Commons when she was elected to the post in 1992.

Women still experience difficulty in being adopted by political parties as parliamentary candidates. The long hours and late sittings at the House of Commons and the great demands made upon an MP's time in dealing with constituency work have also made it difficult to combine family life with a political career. In January 1995 several changes to parliamentary procedure were introduced on an experimental basis, for example sittings of the House of Commons on Wednesday mornings and fewer sittings on Fridays, thus allowing MPs more time in their constituencies. Government business managers also intend to try to reduce the number of late night sittings.

A number of the parliamentary parties are looking to improve the representation of women nationally, for example by taking steps to ensure that more women are included in the lists of candidates available for selection by constituency parties. The Labour Party has taken measures so that candidates are selected from all-women shortlists in half the constituencies where the sitting Labour MP is retiring and in half of the most winnable seats, where Labour needs a swing of 6 per cent or less to win. The constituencies to which these arrangements apply have been decided by a series of regional meetings. The Labour Party has also adopted a system of quotas for representation at all levels, from local branches to the National Executive Committee. For the Liberal Democrats a specified minimum number of candidates must be shortlisted, except where the sitting MP or previous candidate is to be reselected. Shortlists of two to four candidates must include at least one member of each sex (subject to sufficient numbers of applicants) and shortlists of five or more must include at least two members of each sex.

More women are becoming local councillors. According to a study by the Joseph Rowntree Foundation, the proportion of women councillors in Great Britain increased from 17 per cent in 1976 to 25 per cent in 1993. In Northern Ireland women account for 12 per cent of representatives on local authorities.

Women play an active role in the organisations of the political parties at both national and local levels. All the major parties have a women's organisation. In December 1995 women held 14 seats on the 29-member National Executive Committee of the Labour Party (including five women members elected at the party's national conference); 62 of nearly 230 seats on the Conservative Party's National Union Executive Committee; and seven out of 29 seats on the Liberal Democrats' Federal Policy Committee.

Public Appointments

Over 42,000 public appointments are made by departmental ministers to a range of public bodies including operational bodies (such as boards of nationalised industries and health authorities), advisory bodies, tribunals and consumer bodies. The Government's Public Appointments Unit maintains links with women's organisations and seeks to encourage women to serve on these bodies.

In 1991 the Prime Minister announced a government initiative to increase the number of public appointments held by women and by people from ethnic minorities. The Government regards the appointment of more women as beneficial to decision-making and sees women's under-representation as a considerable loss of potential expertise and experience. Its overall objective is that between a quarter and a half of all public appointments will be held by women by the end of 1996. All departments have developed a strategy covering their appointments and those of their non-departmental public bodies. Departmental objectives include improvements to recruitment and selection procedures and the inclusion of women on shortlists.

There has been a gradual increase in the proportion of public appointments held by women, from 19 per cent in 1986 to 23 per cent in 1991, and 30 per cent in 1994. Some departments have a higher percentage; 40 per cent of public appointments made by the Home Office are held by women. Of the new appointments made by public bodies in 1994, nearly half were of women.

Participation in Other Areas

Women are generally playing an increasingly important part in many areas, although in some their involvement remains at a low level, particularly in the more senior posts. A selection of examples is given below. For more information on employment see pp. 45–57.

Business

Industry and commerce have traditionally been male-dominated areas, but more women are beginning to reach senior levels. There has been a steady increase in the proportion of women managers—in spring 1995, 33 per cent of managers and administrators in Great Britain were women. However, at the most senior level, such as chairman, chief executive or managing director, there are very few women, and none of the top 100 companies listed on the Stock Exchange has a female chairman or managing director. Among the women who have achieved high-ranking positions or other success in business are:

—Anita Roddick (founder and chief executive of the Body Shop);

—Aleksandra Clayton (chairman of Alexanders Holdings);

—Ann Gloag (group managing director of Stagecoach Holdings plc);

—Yve Newbold (formerly company secretary of Hanson plc who in 1995 became chief executive of Pro Ned—the organisation which recruits non-executive directors); and

—Jennifer Laing (who became chairman of Saatchi and Saatchi Advertising in April 1995).

The Opportunity 2000 campaign (see p. 54), an employer-led initiative, is aiming to increase women's participation in the workforce including involvement at senior level.

Civil Service

Over half of civil servants are women, but they tend to be concentrated in the lower grades (see p. 59). Nevertheless, the proportion of women in the most senior grades has grown. In 1994 women held nearly 10 per cent of the top posts (grades 1–3) in the Civil Service, as against 4 per cent in 1984.

There are now three women Permanent Secretaries:

—Barbara Mills, head of the Crown Prosecution Service and Director of Public Prosecutions;

—Valerie Strachan, head of Customs and Excise; and

—Ann Bowtell, formerly the first woman to hold the post of First Civil Service Commissioner, and now Permanent Secretary at the Department of Social Security.

Five chief executives of Civil Service executive agencies are women:

—Ann Chant, Child Support Agency;

—Faith Boardman, Contributions Agency;

—Dr Elizabeth McCloy, Occupational Health Service;

—Dr Janet Thompson, Forensic Science Service; and

—Sarah Tyacke, Public Record Office.

Other prominent women at senior levels include Stella Rimington (Director General of the Security Service) and Clare Spottiswoode (Director General of Gas Supply, head of the regulator OFGAS).

Other Public Sector

Large numbers of women are employed in other areas of the public sector, particularly education and health, but tend to be under-represented at senior levels, such as head teacher. In the judiciary women accounted for 47 per cent of lay magistrates in England and Wales in 1995, but fewer than 10 per cent of judges are women (see p. 96). Dame Elizabeth Butler-Sloss, appointed in 1987, became the first woman judge in the Court of Appeal.

Trade Unions

Women account for about a third of trade union membership. They predominate in certain trade unions, such as Unison, the Royal College of Nursing, the National Union of Teachers, and the Union of Shop, Distributive and Allied Workers. In many unions though a disproportionately low number of women become executive council members, full-time officials and delegates to the Trades Union Congress (TUC). Several unions have sought to correct this by positive action, including the operation of reserved seats and quotas for the number of women serving on their decision-making committees. In mid-1995 there were four women general secretaries of TUC-affiliated trade unions: Elizabeth Symons of the Association of First Division Civil Servants, Judy McKnight of the National Association of Probation Officers, Alison Gray of the Writers' Guild of Great Britain, and Rosie Eagleson of the Association of Magisterial Officers. There are, though, more women presidents of trade unions, while a number of unions not affiliated to the TUC have women general secretaries.

Sixteen of the 48 seats on the TUC General Council are held by women. A women's committee advises the TUC on issues relating to women workers, and a TUC women's conference sets the agenda for the committee's work.

Voluntary Sector

Women make an important contribution to the voluntary sector. According to a survey in 1991 of voluntary activity, 53 per cent of volunteers are women, with a particular emphasis in the fields of health and social welfare, and children's education. Several women are chief executives of charities or other national voluntary organisations.

Culture

The contribution of women to British cultural life has broadened in recent years as they have entered areas of artistic activity, such as theatre direction and orchestral conducting, previously occupied mainly by men.

Leading authors include Iris Murdoch, Muriel Spark, P.D. James, Joanna Trollope, Margaret Drabble, A.S. Byatt, Anita Brookner, Catherine Cookson, Pat Barker and Jeanette Winterson.

British actresses have played a distinguished role in the theatre, television and cinema. In 1993 Emma Thompson won an Oscar as the best film actress for her role in *Howard's End*. Other British performers with international reputations include Vanessa Redgrave, Dame Judi Dench, Juliet Stephenson, Helen Mirren, Miranda Richardson, Dame Diana Rigg and Dame Maggie Smith. Deborah Warner is one of Britain's best known theatre directors and Caryl Churchill is one of the leading playwrights to have received international recognition.

Women performers have achieved success in pop and rock music. Kate Bush, Dina Carroll, Annie Lennox, Lisa Stansfield, Des'ree and Eddi Reader are among well-known performers. Barbara Thompson and Annie Whitehead have established strong reputations as jazz musicians.

Government Responsibilities and Strategies

Responsibility for co-ordination of policy on women's issues in Britain has been strengthened. A Ministerial Group on Women's Issues was established in 1987 and in 1992 this was upgraded to a Cabinet Sub-committee for Women's Issues. Individual government departments formulate policies in their specific areas. The Equal Opportunities Commission (EOC) and the Equal Opportunities Commission for Northern Ireland are independent statutory bodies with duties to work towards the elimination of unlawful sex discrimination and marriage discrimination, to promote equality of opportunity between men and women generally, and to keep legislation on sex discrimination and equal pay under review. The Women's National Commission aims to ensure that women's views are given due weight in government.

Cabinet Sub-committee for Women's Issues

With the formation of the Cabinet sub-committee, this was the first occasion on which responsibility for women's issues was allocated to a Cabinet minister. The sub-committee's terms of reference are:

—to review and develop the Government's policy and strategy on issues of concern to women;

—to oversee their implementation; and

—to report as necessary to the Ministerial Committee on Home and Social Affairs.

Membership of the sub-committee comprises ministers with responsibilities for issues of special interest to women, such as health, social security, education and employment, together with ministers responsible for Wales, Scotland and Northern Ireland.

Officials of the Department for Education and Employment's Sex Equality Branch work together with colleagues in other government departments on these issues. In Northern Ireland there is an Interdepartmental Group on Women's Issues.

Equal Opportunities Commissions

The Equal Opportunities Commission (EOC), set up in 1975, has powers to enforce the Sex Discrimination Acts and the Equal Pay Act in Great Britain. It is an independent non-departmental public body funded by a grant from the Department for Education and Employment, amounting to £6 million in 1995–96.

The EOC's statutory duties are to work towards eliminating discrimination and to promote equality of opportunity. It advises people of their legal rights and may give financial or other assistance to help individuals to conduct a case before a court or industrial tribunal.

The EOC also has powers to conduct investigations and to issue notices requiring discriminatory practices to stop. It keeps legislation under review, and undertakes research, educational and publicity work.

Practical advice to employers and others on the best arrangements for implementing equal opportunities policies is given in the EOC's codes of practice relating to elimination of discrimination at work and other matters. In May 1995 it issued for consultation a draft code of practice on pay. The EOC's Equality Exchange, which has 400 member companies, provides an important mecha-

nism to disseminate and exchange information on legal requirements and best practice.

Northern Ireland has its own sex discrimination laws and a
separate commission with similar powers and duties. The Equal
Opportunities Commission for Northern Ireland was set up under
the Sex Discrimination (Northern Ireland) Order 1976. Its funding
for 1995–96 is £1.5 million.

An outline of the sex discrimination and equal opportunities
laws is given on pp. 24–34.

Women's National Commission

The Women's National Commission was set up in 1969 to reflect
the views of women to the Government. It is an independent advisory body with 50 representatives of women's national voluntary
organisations; occupationally based groups, including trade unions
and professional associations; political parties; religious groups;
social, carers and welfare organisations; and ethnic minority
women's organisations. The Commission is chaired jointly by a
government minister (who is also a member of the Cabinet sub-
committee) and by an elected member.

The Commission's aims include:

—bringing to the Government's attention any policies and practices which detract from the quality of women's lives;

—drawing to the attention of member organisations any changes in
government policy and practices which will affect women;

—encouraging women to take an active part in public life; and

—monitoring progress on issues of concern to women.

It organises and participates in seminars and conferences, and
prepares reports, such as the report *In Search of Equality*,

Development and Peace (see Further Reading), the Commission's contribution to Britain's preparations for the UN Conference in Peking. The Commission also produces a range of publications including a *Directory of Women's Organisations* and a handbook *Public Appointments for Women.*

Women's Issues Working Group

In 1992 the Women's Issues Working Group was set up to give personal advice to the then Secretary of State for Employment on practical measures to help women overcome obstacles encountered in the workplace and elsewhere. Among the issues considered by the Group have been the Childcare Initiative (see p. 87), public appointments, problems facing women in the professions, flexible working practices and women returning to work.

In Northern Ireland the Interdepartmental Group on Women's Issues is examining the funding of women's groups in Northern Ireland.

Strategy

The Government's strategy covers a range of areas including support for childcare, public appointments (see p. 13) and the wider consideration of women's interests when policies are being considered. Priorities for action include:

—an extension of local strategies for women to realise their full capabilities (see p. 23);

—a new requirement for Training and Enterprise Councils (TECs) to set and monitor the delivery of equal opportunities;

—the new Family Credit benefit (see p. 81);

—proposals in the longer term for equalising the state pension ages (see p. 85); and

—proposals to speed the hearing of cases of equal pay for work of equal value (see p. 26).

Recent Initiatives

The New Horizons for Women Initiative, a nationwide campaign held in 1993 and 1994, was designed to promote opportunities for women in employment, training and public life. A series of ten regional events culminating in an exhibition in London in November 1994 were attended by nearly 10,900 people.

In Wales the Chwarae Teg (Fair Play) initiative aims to promote and develop the contribution of women to the Welsh economy, encouraging good practice in flexible working, childcare and training opportunities. Among those involved in the initiative are the Welsh Development Agency, TECs, local authorities, the EOC and the Employment Service.

A similar initiative—Fair Play for Women—was launched in England in 1994 jointly by the then Department of Employment and the EOC. Its aim is to help women realise their full capabilities and make a full contribution to the local economy and community. Ten regional consortia, including representatives from the public, private and voluntary sectors, have been set up as local partnerships with support from the Government Offices for the Regions. Each consortium has developed an action plan based on its region's priorities. A similar initiative is planned for Northern Ireland. In Scotland Scottish Enterprise is developing proposals, with the EOC, for a Fair Play Initiative.

The Legal Framework

In most respects women have the same legal rights as men. These rights and duties apply to married as well as to single women. The rights of husbands and wives in respect of property and children are practically equal, and women are entitled to equal treatment in divorce settlements. In general, the criminal law applies equally to men and women, providing the same range of penalties for the same offence, and the same protection to the accused.

The legal framework complies with the relevant article of the Treaty of Rome and with directives covering equal pay and equal treatment in employment and social security in the European Union (see p. 116). The Government strongly supports the steps taken by the EU on equal opportunities, and has put forward a number of proposals. For example, in 1990 it suggested improvements to, and the extension of, a resolution on sexual harassment, which was subsequently adopted by the EU.

Recent advances for women have included:

—enhanced maternity pay and maternity leave arrangements;

—a new system of independent taxation for wives and husbands;

—the right to bring complaints claiming equal pay for work of equal value;

—the recognition that in some circumstances sexual harassment at work may amount to sex discrimination;

—equal retirement ages for women and men working for the same employer; and

—the same occupational pensions and survivors' benefits for women and men in comparable circumstances.

The following legislation applies to Great Britain. Northern Ireland generally has parallel laws.

Equal Pay Act 1970

The purpose of the Equal Pay Act 1970 is to eliminate discrimination between men and women in Great Britain on pay and other conditions of employment, such as overtime, bonuses, and holiday and sick-leave entitlement. The Act, which came into force in December 1975, established the right to equal pay if a woman is employed in work which is the same as, or broadly similar to, that of a man; or in a job which, although different from that of a man, has been given an equal value under a job evaluation scheme. The Act was widened in 1984 to allow a woman to claim equal pay for work of equal value where no job evaluation study has been conducted.

If a woman considers that she is entitled to equal pay, she can raise the matter with her employer or trade union. If agreement cannot be reached with the employer, she can seek help from the independent Advisory, Conciliation and Arbitration Service, and ultimately go to an industrial tribunal for a decision. Industrial tribunals may refer a case to an independent expert who will prepare a report on the relative value of the two jobs under comparison.

Developments in case law relating to the Act which are beneficial to women include:

—establishing the importance of analytical job evaluation in equal value cases; and

—the right for a woman claiming equal pay to have each individual term of contract considered and uprated to that of a comparable male even if her overall remuneration package is greater than his.

Concern has been expressed though about delays in cases brought under the equal pay for work of equal value provisions. The Government shares this concern, and measures to address these delays are being taken, including simplifying and speeding up industrial tribunal procedures.

Sex Discrimination Act 1975

The Sex Discrimination Act 1975, as amended by the Sex Discrimination Act 1986 and the Employment Act 1989, makes discrimination between men and women on the grounds of sex unlawful in employment and training; education; the provision of goods, facilities and services; and in the disposal and management of premises. The Act gives individuals a right of direct access to the civil courts—county courts in England and Wales and the Sheriff Court in Scotland—and industrial tribunals for legal remedies for unlawful discrimination.

The Act defines two types of discrimination:

—direct discrimination, which arises when a person is treated less favourably than another on the grounds of his or her sex; and

—indirect discrimination, involving the application of conditions which, though equal in a formal sense, in practice favour one sex or the other.

For a claim of direct discrimination to be valid, the circumstances of the man and woman must be similar. If a sex discrimination complaint is successful, the tribunal may award compensation, declare the rights of the parties and recommend that employers take specific action to reduce or remove the effect of discrimination, such as reinstatement for employees dismissed on discriminatory grounds.

Employment and Training

It is unlawful for an employer to discriminate in arrangements for recruiting and engaging employees, and in the treatment of employees in matters such as promotion, training, transfer and dismissal. Training may be given under the Act on a single-sex basis for work in which comparatively few members of one sex were engaged over the previous 12 months, to encourage individuals of that sex to take advantage of opportunities for doing such work, and for people who have not been working because of domestic or family responsibilities.

Education

Education providers—schools, colleges, universities and local education authorities—have a general duty to ensure that their facilities are available without sex discrimination. It is unlawful for a co-educational school, college or university to discriminate regarding attendance; a college cannot, for example, decide to admit a certain quota of men or women irrespective of their qualifications. This stipulation does not apply to single-sex schools or colleges. Once admitted to a co-educational establishment, pupils must have equal access to the curriculum and equal opportunities to use the facilities available. A girl cannot, for instance, be refused entry to a woodwork class on the grounds of gender, and similarly a boy cannot be refused entry to a home economics course. The Act does not prohibit the provision of separate facilities for boys and girls where these are considered appropriate, for example, in physical education. It is permissible to offer single-sex classes in subjects where research shows that single-sex groups attain better results.

Other Aspects

People providing goods, facilities and services must not discriminate against a woman either by refusing them or by supplying them on less favourable terms than to a man. It is unlawful, with certain exceptions, to discriminate when selling or letting land, houses, flats and business premises.

It is unlawful to publish, or place for publication, advertisements which are discriminatory, or which indicate an intention to discriminate. A job advertisement using a description such as 'waiter', 'salesman' or 'steward' must point out that both men and women are eligible.

Sex Discrimination Act 1986

The Sex Discrimination Act 1986 was designed to bring British law into line with the European Community (EC) directive on equal treatment and to remove sex discrimination in British employment legislation.

Under the 1975 Act, private households and businesses with five or fewer employees had been exempted from the requirement not to discriminate. The 1986 Act provided for a more limited exemption for private households, while the exemption for firms employing five or fewer people was removed. It also outlawed discriminatory elements in collective agreements, internal rules of undertakings, and rules governing independent occupations and professions. It lifted legal restrictions on hours of work which prevented women from working shifts and at night. Under the Act, women have the right to continue working until the same age as men in those occupations that have different retirement ages for men and women.

Employment Act 1989

The Employment Act 1989 reduced the extent of the exceptions allowed in discrimination on grounds of sex in employment. The ban on women working underground in mines and quarries was removed, as were some restrictions on working with machinery in factories. Nevertheless, protection is retained in special cases such as work which, through exposure to radiation or lead, might endanger the health of an unborn child. Women also became eligible to receive statutory redundancy payments up to the same age—65— as men.

Rights of Pregnant Workers

The Employment Protection Act 1975 gave important rights to a working woman expecting a baby. Women with two years' service working for more than 16 hours a week, and women with five years' service employed for between eight and 16 hours a week had the right not to be unfairly dismissed because of pregnancy, except in limited circumstances, and also had an entitlement to return to work not later than 29 weeks after the birth of the baby. Under the Employment Act 1980, women employees who are pregnant cannot be unreasonably refused time off for antenatal care and must be paid for the time off.

New rights for women were implemented in Great Britain in 1994 under the Trade Union Reform and Employment Rights Act 1993. The dismissal of a pregnant worker because of her pregnancy or for associated reasons became automatically unfair. The Act also significantly extends and enhances maternity rights. A pregnant employee now has the right to 14 weeks' statutory maternity leave, regardless of length of service or the number of hours worked in a week. During this period all non-wage contractual benefits must be continued. In addition to the new rights under the 1993 Act, women with two years of continuous service—who account for over two-thirds of women employees—continued to have the right to return to work within 29 weeks of the birth, giving them entitlement to up to around 40 weeks' maternity absence. This represents one of the longest periods of maternity absence in Europe. Regulations which came into effect in February 1995 (see p. 34) ensured part-time employees' entitlement to this longer absence on the same basis as full-time employees.

Details of the statutory maternity pay scheme and other maternity benefits are given on pp. 77–9.

Similar provisions are in force in Northern Ireland.

Social Security

The Social Security Pensions Act 1975 introduced the State Earnings Related Pension Scheme, under which women earners receive the same benefits as men. It also laid down that women should have equal access to occupational pension schemes with regard to age and length of service. Unequal treatment persists, however, in certain occupational schemes in terms of access to, and levels of benefit for, part-time workers. The Act also protects the entitlement to the basic pension for people unable to work because of domestic responsibilities, such as care of elderly and invalid relatives.

The Social Security Act 1980 provides for equality of entitlement to personal social security benefits, allowances for dependent children, and short-term National Insurance benefits for dependent adults. Women thus have the same right as men to claim unemployment and sickness benefit for their spouses and children.

Immigration and Nationality

The rights of women under immigration and nationality laws were extended by the British Nationality Act 1981, and are now substantially the same as those enjoyed by men. Women gained the right to transmit British citizenship, on equal terms with men, to their children born overseas. A woman who is a British citizen or otherwise settled in Britain may be joined by her spouse or fiancé if he meets the requirements of the Immigration Rules.

Matrimonial and Family Law

Reforms to matrimonial and family law have been implemented in recent years. In England and Wales, the Matrimonial and Family Proceedings Act 1984 relaxed the time restrictions on the presentation of divorce petitions and reformed the legal framework for making financial settlements on divorce. These changes were designed to give the courts further scope to deal with the problems which arise on marital breakdown. The relevant law applies equally to both spouses. One of the primary objectives of the Family Law Reform Act 1987 was to remove legal discrimination against children born outside marriage. The Act also made it easier to obtain maintenance for such children from absent parents. The Children Act 1989 reformed child law, including that relating to custody and guardianship, and emphasised the responsibility of both parents for their children. Rape within marriage was confirmed as unlawful by the House of Lords in 1991 following a ruling by the Court of Appeal.

In Scotland the Family Law (Scotland) Act 1985 was designed to promote greater fairness and consistency in financial provision on divorce, and clarified the law on the property rights and legal capacity of married couples. Legislation in 1986 removed or amended provisions which discriminated against illegitimate children and their parents.

Changes are planned by the Government in connection with divorce in England and Wales. Already in Scotland the courts must take into account at the time of a divorce the accrued rights in occupational and personal pension schemes when assessing the division of assets between husband and wife, and to divide assets fairly according to a set of principles set out in the 1985 Act. Provisions in the Pensions Act 1995 (see pp. 84–5) may, where appropriate, give a divorced wife the right to a share of her husband's pension rights on retirement, although the legislation would not be retrospective. Proposals to reform the divorce laws in England and Wales were contained in a White Paper published in April 1995 (see Further Reading). Couples would have to wait for at least a year after filing proceedings before they could obtain a divorce, and during this period they would be encouraged to use mediation services. The sole ground for divorce would be that the marriage had broken down irretrievably.

Personal Taxation

Since April 1990, when a system of independent taxation was introduced, husbands and wives have been treated as separate individuals for tax purposes. They are taxed on their own income, and can claim their own tax allowances. Prior to independent taxation, a married woman's income was treated as her husband's for tax purposes. This meant that married women did not have independence and privacy in their own tax affairs, and some couples paid more tax simply because they were married.

Everyone is entitled to a personal allowance, whether male or female, married or single. This is an amount of income which a person can receive each year before he or she has to pay tax. It is set at £3,525 for the 1995–96 tax year. In addition, a married couple can get the married couple's allowance. This is set at £1,720 but is restricted to give relief at the 15 per cent rate, so that it reduces the amount of tax that has to be paid by £258. A couple can choose which partner receives the allowance or they may divide it between them. A single parent is able to claim the additional personal allowance which is worth the same as the married couple's allowance. Husbands and wives are also taxed independently on their capital gains.

Rights of Part-time Workers

Many employment rights—such as those relating to health and safety, race and sex discrimination, trade union membership and activities, unlawful deductions from wages and time off for antenatal care—have long applied to all employees, regardless of hours of work or length of service. In order to qualify for some employment rights, however, employees have to satisfy certain conditions, such as having two years' continuous service for rights on unfair dismissal and to redundancy payments. In February 1995 the Employment Protection (Part-time Employees) Regulations 1995 took effect. These give part-time employees—a large majority of whom are women (see p. 46)—entitlement to all the statutory employment rights on the same basis as full-time employees. This change followed a judicial review case in the House of Lords. Previously part-time employees working between eight and 16 hours a week had had to complete five years' continuous service with the same employer to be eligible for unfair dismissal and redundancy payment rights. Those working less than eight hours a week could never qualify. The Government is monitoring the effects of the changes on the creation of part-time jobs.

Education

The Government is committed to promoting equal opportunities in schools, colleges and universities and to encouraging greater participation by girls and young women in traditionally male-dominated disciplines such as science, engineering and technology. It helps to promote equal opportunities by monitoring participation and providing guidance for school governors, college governors and others on the legislative requirements. Charters for further education and higher education—issued under the Government's Citizen's Charter Initiative—call for educational institutions to set out policies for equal opportunities.

Significant advances in recent years include:

—a large increase in women in further and higher education;

—reforms in the school curriculum;

—more part-time higher and further education courses; and

—expansion in access courses and the accreditation of prior learning.

Qualifications

Between 1975 and 1992 the proportion of adults in Great Britain with qualifications at or above GCSE (General Certificate of Secondary Education) grades A to C or equivalent nearly doubled from 27 to 53 per cent. Although more men than women have such qualifications, the difference has narrowed. For example, in 1975, 31 per cent of men and 22 per cent of women had such a qualification, but by 1992 the proportions had grown to 55 and 49 per cent respectively.

Since the early 1980s the number of women gaining a higher education qualification in Britain has more than doubled, reaching 172,000 in 1991–92 (see Table 4). More men achieve a higher education qualification, but the gap has narrowed and women accounted for 46 per cent of such qualifications achieved in 1991–92.

Table 4: Higher Education Qualifications Achieved in Britain

	1980–81	1985–86	1991–92
Men	144,000	158,000	204,000
Women	78,000	103,000	172,000
Per cent achieved by women	*35*	*39*	*46*

Source: Department for Education and Employment.

Schools

Full-time attendance at school is obligatory for both girls and boys between the ages of five (four in Northern Ireland) and 16. A growing proportion of children under five attend nursery schools and classes and infants' classes in primary schools. In 1994, 728,000 children under five received pre-primary school education, 56 per cent of this age group, compared with 28 per cent in 1975. Many more were in day nurseries or playgroups (now known as pre-schools). In July 1995 the Government launched a voucher scheme to provide a pre-school place for every four-year-old in Britain whose parents wish to take it up. The first pre-school places under the scheme will become available from April 1996 in a limited number of areas, with the scheme being fully available from April 1997.

Boys and girls are taught together in most primary schools. Over 80 per cent of pupils in state secondary schools in England and Wales and 64 per cent in Northern Ireland attend mixed schools, while nearly all secondary schools in Scotland are mixed. Most independent schools for younger children are mixed. Independent schools providing secondary education are mostly single-sex, although there is a trend towards mixed schools, including some of the well-known public schools which formerly admitted only boys.

School Curriculum

Major reforms have been made to the school curriculum. The introduction of the National Curriculum in England and Wales has established a minimum educational entitlement for all pupils and is considered a major advance in equal opportunities. It ensures that girls in England and Wales have access to the same broad and balanced curriculum as boys up to the age of 16, thereby removing discrimination and stereotyping in subject choice, and providing all pupils with a similar foundation for further and higher education, training and employment. The National Curriculum prescribes core and foundation subjects to be studied.[3] In science, one of the core subjects, boys and girls must study physics and chemistry as well as biology. In technology all pupils must have the opportunity to use hard construction materials, such as wood and metal, as well as food and textiles.

Subjects such as personal and social education can help to combat sex discrimination and stereotyping, encouraging positive

[3] Details of the National Curriculum are given in *Education* (Aspects of Britain: HMSO, 1995).

changes in attitude. Schools must ensure that their programmes of work-related activities are free of stereotyping and that they pay attention to equal opportunities.

Parallel reforms have been carried out in Scotland and Northern Ireland. In Scotland the content and management of the curriculum are not statutorily prescribed, but the Secretary of State issues guidance to education authorities, based mainly on advice from HM Inspectorate of Schools and the Scottish Consultative Council on the Curriculum. In October 1993 the Council issued two booklets on equal opportunities to all education authorities and schools in Scotland. This guidance encourages the promotion of equal opportunities in all school activities and equal access to all subjects in the curriculum.

Examination Results

Examination results show a progressive reduction in sex stereotyping in schools as well as a steady improvement in the performance of girls in examinations. Among school-leavers girls outperform boys, especially in Scotland where over 49 per cent of girls in 1993–94 achieved one or more Scottish Certificate of Education (SCE) Highers, compared with 39 per cent of boys, and 20 per cent of girls achieved five or more Highers, as opposed to 16 per cent of boys.

Between 1985 and 1994 the proportion of 15-year-old girls achieving at least one GCSE (grade A to C) or a higher qualification rose from 59 to 75 per cent, while there was an increase for boys from 53 to 64 per cent.[4] Many fewer girls aged 15 now achieve no

---

[4] Figures relate to different examinations. The GCSE was introduced in September 1986 with the first examinations in 1988. It replaced the previous two-tier system of the Certificate of Secondary Education and the General Certificate of Education (GCE).

qualification; only 7 per cent of girls leaving in 1994 had no GCSE/SCE standard grade passes.

The introduction of the GCSE, first taken in 1988, led to a marked improvement in the number of girls taking and passing 16+ examinations in science, computing and technology. In 1994, 41 per cent of girls aged 16 had achieved a GCSE at grade A to C in at least one science subject, compared with 26 per cent in 1987—the equivalent figures for boys were 40 and 34 per cent. Girls have been similarly successful in mathematics. There are a number of initiatives designed to encourage greater involvement by girls and women in science and technology (see pp. 50–1).

Careers Education and Guidance

Schools and the careers service also have an important role to play in helping young people to fulfil their potential through the provision of careers education and guidance. Effective careers education and guidance provides pupils with information about the widest possible range of careers opportunities and challenges negative gender/career stereotypes. The Government is funding a number of initiatives which will enhance provision for careers education and guidance, including a new Grants for Education Support and Training programme which will provide over £4 million for the training of careers teachers in over 100 local education authorities in England in 1995–96.

The Government is funding a number of other initiatives aimed at improving teacher competence and disseminating good practice. It has also taken steps to ensure that young people and their parents are aware of the importance of careers education and guidance and what they can expect schools and the careers service to provide.

Further and Higher Education

One of the Government's priorities for student recruitment in further and higher education[5] is to provide more opportunities for women, particularly for mature students with domestic responsibilities. Measures designed to encourage female recruitment include improving guidance and information about opportunities and promoting more flexible forms of provision such as open learning schemes. In addition, from 1995–96 the Further Education Funding Council is compensating further education institutions for the costs incurred in securing the provision of childcare facilities for certain groups of people on low incomes.

Student Numbers

There has been a considerable rise in the number of students in higher education, particularly of female students. Between 1970–71 and 1992–93 the number of female full-time student enrolments rose from 182,000 to 460,000 and female part-time enrolments from 23,000 to 224,000. The proportion of female full-time and part-time enrolments was 47 per cent in 1992–93 (see Table 5), compared with 33 per cent in 1970–71.

As in schools, women are strongly represented on arts and other courses such as education, but less strongly in science and technology. In 1992–93 more than twice as many female as male home students enrolled on arts courses, but the position was virtually reversed for science (see Table 6). In social studies enrolments were more evenly split.

---

[5] Under the Education Reform Act 1988, higher education comprises courses of a standard higher than GCE Advanced level or its equivalent, and further education all other post-school courses.

Table 5: Enrolments in Higher Education 1992–93

	Men '000s	Women '000s	Per cent women
Full-time and sandwich enrolments:			
Universities:			
Undergraduates	191	166	*46*
Postgraduates	48	31	*39*
Other[a]:			
Undergraduates	245	250	*51*
Postgraduates	13	13	*50*
Total full-time	**497**	**461**	*48*
Part-time enrolments:			
Universities:			
Undergraduates	6	9	*60*
Postgraduates	35	26	*43*
Open University[b]	53	52	*50*
Other[a]:			
Undergraduates	144	116	*45*
Postgraduates	24	21	*47*
Total part-time	**262**	**224**	*46*
Total enrolments	**759**	**685**	*47*

Source: Department for Education and Employment.

[a] Including polytechnics and colleges which became universities in 1993–94.

[b] Figures relate to 1993.

Note: Differences between totals and the sums of their component parts are due to rounding.

Over 4 million students were enrolled on further education courses in 1992–93. More women than men are enrolled on further education courses, with about two-thirds of older students being women.

Table 6: First Degree Full-time and Sandwich Home Student Enrolments in Higher Education 1992–93

	Men '000s	Women '000s	Total '000s	Per cent women
Arts	55	112	167	67
Science	158	85	242	35
Social studies	70	72	143	50
Other	46	58	104	56
Total enrolments	**330**	**328**	**657**	**50**

Sources: Department for Education and Employment, Welsh Office, The Scottish Office Education Department and Department of Education, Northern Ireland.

Note: Differences between totals and the sums of their component parts are due to rounding.

Access Courses

'Access' courses, providing more part-time and flexible learning programmes and with fewer formal entry requirements, have helped to support the growing participation by women in further and higher education. Some access courses are designed specifically to help women gain entry to subjects where they have traditionally been under-represented, for example architecture, electronics, information technology, mathematics and science.

Access courses have increased in number; in higher education the number rose from 130 in 1984 to over 1,200 in 1994–95.

Return to Learning courses are particularly popular among women, and provide a route to academic and vocational qualifications.

Open and Distance Learning

The growth of open and distance learning—learning undertaken without the direct supervision of a tutor, through the use of various media such as television—has helped to bring higher and further education within the range of large numbers of women.

A major event in open learning was the establishment in 1969 of the Open University. Just under half of students on its non-residential undergraduate and other courses in 1994 were women. The University is particularly suited to women's needs with its flexible study hours and course arrangements, enabling students to organise study around their normal working and domestic circumstances.

Women in Teaching

Teaching in primary and secondary schools has traditionally been an area where women are well represented. In 1993, 65 per cent of teachers in state schools in England and Wales were women: over 81 per cent in primary schools and nearly 50 per cent in secondary schools. In Scotland and Northern Ireland about 70 and 65 per cent respectively of teachers are women.

Fewer head teachers, though, are women. In England and Wales in 1993 just over 50 per cent of head teachers in nursery and primary schools and about 22 per cent in secondary schools were women. One factor is the differences in the age profile and the length of service—women teachers are generally younger and more men have long experience of teaching. However, the proportion of promotions to head teacher going to women is increasing; in 1992–93, 76 per cent of promotions to head or deputy head in primary schools and 37 per cent in secondary schools went to women.

Fewer women work in further and higher education, but the proportion of full-time women academic staff in universities grew from 14 per cent in 1980–81 to 22 per cent in 1992–93.

Employment

In the last ten years the number of women in employment has increased by about 1.5 million, with growth in both full-time and part-time employment. The Government is fully committed to equality of opportunity in employment and the principle of equal pay. It believes that every woman with the ability and who wishes to work should have the chance to progress as far and as fully at work as possible.

Economic Activity

Women account for a growing proportion—nearly 46 per cent in 1995—of the workforce in employment, which includes both employees and the self-employed. Britain has one of the highest rates in the European Union for women's participation in employment. The proportion of women employees has steadily increased (see Table 7), and accounted in 1995 for over 49 per cent of employees. On the other hand, women represent a much lower proportion of the self-employed—around 24 per cent.

The economically active population comprises those aged 16 and over who are either in employment or are unemployed but looking for a job. In spring 1995 the economic activity rate for women in Great Britain was 53 per cent, compared with 73 per cent for men. Looking at the population of working age (16–59 for women and 16–64 for men), the equivalent rates were 71 per cent and 85 per cent respectively.

Table 7: Women in Employment in Britain

Thousands, seasonally adjusted, June

	1985	1990	1992	1993	1994	1995
Employees in employment	9,506	10,858	10,677	10,636	10,717	10,844
Self-employed	677	842	782	794	811	803
HM Forces	16	18	20	19	18	16
Work-related government training programmes	76	163	120	117	111	100
Total women in employment	10,275	11,881	11,599	11,566	11,657	11,764
Total workforce in employment	24,683	27,186	25,738	25,348	25,478	25,730
Women employees in employment as per cent of total employees	*44.4*	*47.4*	*48.7*	*49.3*	*49.5*	*49.5*
Women in self-employment as per cent of total self-employed	*24.5*	*23.7*	*24.3*	*25.0*	*24.7*	*24.0*

Source: Central Statistical Office.

Around 6.3 million women in Great Britain work full-time and 5 million part-time (see Table 8). The large majority of women who work part time do this because they wish to do so and only a small proportion because they cannot find a full-time job. In spring 1995 women accounted for 33 per cent of full-time employees and self-employed, compared with 29 per cent in 1984, and for 82 per cent of part-time workers. More women and men now have second jobs. Around 744,000 women had a second job in spring 1995, and since the mid-1980s more women than men have held second jobs.

In the European Union only Britain, Finland and Sweden have a lower unemployment rate for women than for men. In spring 1995 the unemployment rate for women in Britain, using the International Labour Organisation measure, was 7 per cent, compared with 10.1 per cent for men. About one-third of the unemployed in Britain are women.

Table 8: Full-time and Part-time Employment in Great Britain

Thousands, seasonally adjusted

	Spring 1984	Spring 1989	Spring 1992	Spring 1993	Spring 1994	Spring 1995
Full-time workers	18,395	20,037	19,343	18,973	19,009	19,256
of whom: men	13,050	13,807	13,051	12,737	12,800	12,954
women	5,346	6,230	6,292	6,236	6,209	6,302
Per cent women	*28.9*	*31.1*	*32.5*	*32.9*	*32.7*	*32.7*
Part-time workers in main job	4,851	5,541	5,898	5,971	6,118	6,146
of whom: men	558	719	978	1,004	1,081	1,126
women	4,292	4,823	4,920	4,967	5,036	5,020
Per cent women	*88.5*	*87.0*	*83.4*	*83.2*	*82.3*	*81.7*

Source: *Labour Force Survey*.

Employment by Sector

Women have traditionally been concentrated in certain types of job and industries, especially service industries (see Table 9). In spring 1995 around 84 per cent of women in Great Britain were working in services, compared with 59 per cent of men.

The pattern of employment by sector varies considerably. Women represented 54 per cent of service workers in Great Britain in spring 1995, but only 28 per cent of those in manufacturing and 10 per cent in construction. Within the services sector there was a large variation in the employment of women. In transport and communications only 22 per cent were women, but women accounted for over 68 per cent of those working in public administration, education and health.

Table 9: Employment by Sector in Great Britain Spring 1995

Thousands, not seasonally adjusted

	Men	Women	Total	Per cent women
Agriculture and fishing	362	136	498	*27.3*
Energy and water supply	264	63	327	*19.3*
Manufacturing	3,467	1,346	4,813	*28.0*
Construction	1,604	174	1,778	*9.8*
Services	8,252	9,565	17,817	*53.7*
All employees and self-employed	14,028	11,321	25,350	*44.7*

Source: *Labour Force Survey.*

Occupations

In spring 1995 about 7.9 million women in Great Britain were in non-manual occupations, compared with 3.4 million in manual occupations (see Table 10). Women tend to work in a more limited range of occupations than men. Women remain concentrated in occupations such as clerical or secretarial jobs, personal services such as nursing or care assistants, in sales occupations, and in professional occupations such as health professionals and teachers. Recent research by the EOC has indicated that job segregation in workplaces remains extensive, with some jobs being done largely by men and others by women. It found that clerical and administrative workers tended to be women, but skilled workers, senior professional, technical and managerial staff were predominantly men. Over half of workplaces employed only male managers.

Table 10: Employment by Occupation in Great Britain Spring 1995

Thousands, not seasonally adjusted

	Men	Women	Total	Per cent women
Managers and administrators	2,749	1,346	4,095	*32.9*
Professional occupations	1,565	1,047	2,612	*40.1*
Associate professional and technical occupations	1,214	1,137	2,352	*48.3*
Clerical occupations	933	2,862	3,795	*75.4*
Craft and related occupations	2,873	323	3,196	*10.1*
Personal and protective services	896	1,729	2,625	*65.9*
Selling	715	1,259	1,974	*63.8*
Plant and machine operatives	1,952	478	2,430	*19.7*
Other occupations	1,044	1,097	2,141	*51.2*
All employees and self-employed[a]	14,028	11,321	25,350	*44.7*
of which:				
Manual	*6,744*	*3,394*	*10,138*	*33.5*
Non-manual	*7,070*	*7,880*	*14,950*	*52.7*

Source: *Labour Force Survey*.

[a] Includes people who did not state their occupation.

Nevertheless, there are several professions where more women are working. For example:

—women lawyers increased from 8,000 in 1984 to 28,000 in 1994, representing 31 per cent of the profession; and

—women chartered accountants grew from 19,000 in 1984 to 39,000 in 1994—23 per cent of chartered accountants.

Science and Technology

Women remain significantly under-represented in science, technology and engineering. Among the initiatives helping to tackle this are:

—The Teaching Company Scheme, which provides industrially relevant training for young graduates over a two-year period while they undertake key technology transfer projects in companies under the joint supervision of academic and company staff. Over 500 partnerships are in progress; by March 1993, 22 per cent of graduates working on the scheme were women.

—Women in Technology, a private sector initiative which encourages women to enter or return to careers in information technology. In recent years it has organised 3,500 workshops for employers and has established a database for women returners.

The Government attaches great importance to promoting the participation of women in science, engineering and technology. In 1993 it established an independent committee to consider ways in which the potential, skills and expertise of women could best be utilised, particularly for the benefit of science, engineering and technology. Its report, *The Rising Tide—A Report on Women in Science, Engineering and Technology* (see Further Reading), was published in February 1994. In December 1994 the Development Unit on Women in Science, Engineering and Technology was set up in the Office of Science and Technology (OST, now part of the Department of Trade and Industry) as a focus for a campaign to increase women's participation. It has begun to take steps to raise awareness of the contribution which women can make to science, engineering and technology; to ensure access to adequate careers advice; and to promote good employment practices. OST funding of 12 Royal Society Dorothy Hodgkin fellowships is designed to help retain some of the best women in science.

Earnings

Men continue to receive higher average earnings than women, although there has been a significant narrowing of the gap since the Equal Pay Act 1970. Nevertheless, a recent EOC report found that at least 4 million women in Britain were low paid, and that low pay was a key issue in the failure of women to achieve equality.

Before the Equal Pay Act, women's full-time average hourly earnings were 63 per cent of those of men. By spring 1995, according to the Labour Force Survey, full-time employees in Great Britain earned on average:

—£8.30 an hour for men and £6.60 for women, so that women's rates were 79 per cent of those of men; and

—£350 a week for men and £247 for women, so that women's gross weekly earnings were 71 per cent of those of men.

The greater difference for weekly earnings reflects the longer hours worked by men; in spring 1995, average hours for full-time employees and the self-employed were 41.6 for men and 35.1 for women. Hourly earnings of men (including part-time workers) are higher than those of women in all occupations, although there is a wide variation in the difference by type of occupation. Women's earnings as a proportion of those of men are greatest in professional occupations and smallest in sales occupations.

In the second half of the 1980s many companies, such as some of the largest retailers, undertook job evaluation studies which led to some women's jobs being upgraded. The Government believes that this is a significant development which should encourage a further narrowing of the pay gap between men and women.

Self-employment

Self-employment has generally been growing among both women and men, although the numbers of self-employed declined during the recession of the early 1990s. Fewer women than men are self-employed—about 7 per cent of women, compared with 18 per cent of men. By June 1995 there were 803,000 self-employed women in Britain, 20 per cent more than in 1985. Among self-employed women nearly three-quarters are sole traders and just over a quarter are employers. Most women setting up in business do so in retailing, hotels and catering, or financial services.

Women may often face barriers when starting up in business, such as experiencing greater difficulty in raising capital as they are less likely to have property to offer as security, or to have management experience or formal qualifications. The Government is committed to encouraging those who wish to start their own business. Advice is available through the new network of Business Links, which are being set up to bring together in a single point of access organisations supporting enterprise, such as local companies, Training and Enterprise Councils (TECs, see p. 55), chambers of commerce, local authorities and enterprise agencies.[6] In Scotland arrangements for providing integrated business advice are slightly different, with Local Enterprise Companies (LECs, see p. 55) playing a significant role, while several local Business Information Centres have been opened.

The Business Start Up scheme provides help to unemployed people setting up their own business, and in 1992–93 women accounted for 31 per cent of those assisted. This scheme is available through TECs and LECs. They also provide other support for women in enterprise including networks, or women's business clubs, providing a forum for discussing and promoting the interests of women in business; help for women returners; and arranging the provision of childcare facilities.

Flexible Working Arrangements

The Government is encouraging the adoption by employers of flexible working arrangements for both men and women. It believes that flexible working can help employers to:

—recruit and retain able and skilled staff;

—match their staffing to cope with peaks and troughs in the level of business; and

—reduce overheads.

Employers are increasingly using flexible working arrangements such as part-time employment, job sharing, flexible working hours, career break schemes and homeworking.

Homeworking including teleworking—people working from home using information technology—is becoming more extensive.

[6] For further information on Business Links see *Government and Industry* (Aspects of Britain: HMSO, 1995).

Over 70 per cent of those working at home in Great Britain in 1993 were women. Apart from information technology, many work in various professional, clerical, secretarial and selling jobs; only a minority are engaged in manufacturing and this appears to be becoming less significant.

Opportunity 2000

Opportunity 2000 is an employer-led initiative launched in 1991 to increase the quantity and quality of women's participation in the workforce. Over 280 employers employing 25 per cent of the work-force are members, mainly large private and public sector organisa-tions. When joining Opportunity 2000, members agree to set specific goals for increasing women's opportunities at work and to arrange for progress to be measured regularly.

In its third report, published in 1994, details are given of improvements by members to their equal opportunities' policies and practices. For example:

—58 per cent of member organisations offer job share arrange-ments to all employees, compared with 33 per cent in 1993;

—60 per cent offer flexible working hours, as against 32 per cent in 1993;

—25 per cent offer school-term contracts;

—71 per cent offer maternity arrangements above the statutory minimum;

—67 per cent offer paternity leave;

—92 per cent provide ongoing training for part-time staff;

—23 per cent offer homeworking, compared with 8 per cent in 1993; and

—31 per cent have initiatives to develop paths out of jobs traditionally occupied by women, such as secretarial work.

More members are now monitoring progress on equal opportunities in numerical terms, tracking the proportion of women at various levels within their organisation. About a third of members have reviewed criteria for recruitment and also promotion and performance-related pay arrangements to ensure that there is no gender bias.

Training

The Government is committed to ensuring that there are training opportunities which address the specific needs of women. Since 1990 the network of 81 Training and Enterprise Councils in England and Wales and 22 Local Enterprise Companies in Scotland has been responsible for the delivery of the Government's training, enterprise and vocational education programmes.[7] TECs and LECs are employer-led bodies. In Northern Ireland training is the responsibility of the Training and Employment Agency.

TECs and LECs are required to ensure equal opportunities in all their activities and to ensure that training providers promote equal opportunities. TECs are required to set out an equal opportunities strategy with a plan for implementation and arrangements to monitor progress. In Northern Ireland the Training and Employment Agency is committed to supporting the elimination of all forms of unlawful discrimination in employment.

TECs are also responsible for implementing the Investors in People initiative. This is based on a rigorous national standard

[7] For more information on training programmes see *Employment* (Aspects of Britain: HMSO, 1994).

which helps companies to improve their performance by linking the training and development of all staff—men and women, and part-time as well as full-time staff—directly to the achievement of business objectives. By mid-1995 nearly 2,100 had achieved the standard and over 18,900 had made a formal commitment to work towards it.

Among the main training programmes in Great Britain are:

— Training for Work, which aims to help long-term unemployed people to find jobs and improve their work-related skills. TECs and LECs offer a wide range of opportunities for women, including back-to-work foundation courses, updating for professional people to return to work after a career break, and career development for women at management level. Around a third of enrolments are women, and more women than men have obtained a job or have gone on to further or higher education at the end of training.

— Modern Apprenticeships, Youth Training and Youth Credits, under which credits can be presented to an employer or training provider in exchange for training. In Scotland the Skillseekers scheme is equivalent to Youth Credits. About two-fifths of trainees on Youth Training/Youth Credits are women.

— Career Development Loans, which help individuals to pay for vocational training through loans available from four banks with help from the Government to cover interest payments. Women account for a growing proportion of those receiving loans—35 per cent in 1993–94.

National Training Awards aim to complement the activities of TECs and LECs by promoting good training practice, rewarding companies which have carried out exceptionally effective training.

Vocational Qualifications

New National Vocational Qualifications (NVQs) have been established in England, Wales and Northern Ireland, while in Scotland parallel Scottish Vocational Qualifications (SVQs) are in place. NVQs and SVQs are designed mainly for people in the workplace, although they can also be studied full time. They are job-specific, based on national standards of competence set by industry and are assessed in the workplace.

General National Vocational Qualifications (GNVQs) were introduced in 1992 for young people in full-time education between the ages of 16 and 18. They provide a broad-based foundation from which students can progress either to further and higher education or into employment and further training. General Scottish Vocational Qualifications (GSVQs), which are broadly comparable with GNVQs, are designed to meet the needs of those aged 16 to 19 at school or in further education colleges.

NVQs, GNVQs, SVQs and GSVQs are designed to allow equal access for both women and men. Some can be studied part time and offer flexible modes of learning and assessment. These qualifications also provide the opportunity for accreditation of prior learning—skills and abilities developed in previous jobs or elsewhere such as voluntary work.

The Civil Service and the Public Sector

The first formal Programme for Action to achieve equality of opportunity for women in the Civil Service was introduced in 1984. Since then there have been considerable changes in the operation of the Civil Service, notably with the creation of over 100 executive agencies and a significant move away from centralised control.[8] Accordingly, a revised Programme for Action was launched in 1992, providing a policy framework within which departments and agencies can develop equal opportunities strategies tailored to their operational needs. Most departments and agencies have adopted action plans and many have set equal opportunity 'benchmarks' for women.

Progress Report

According to the latest progress report published in March 1995 (see Further Reading), the proportion of women increased to 51 per cent in 1994 (see Table 11). Although recruitment of women has not risen, the leaving rate for women has fallen considerably and is now below that for men. In addition, the resignation rate which used to be 2.5 times that of men has dropped very substantially.

[8] For further information see *The Civil Service* (Aspects of Britain: HMSO, 1995).

Table 11: Women in the Home Civil Service by Grade Level

	1984		1994	
	Number	Per cent	Number	Per cent
Grade 1	0	*0*	2	*5.7*
Grade 2	5	*3.7*	9	*7.4*
Grade 3	25	*4.7*	48	*10.1*
Grade 4	11	*3.4*	35	*9.4*
Grade 5	173	*6.6*	379	*13.3*
Grade 6	380	*7.7*	674	*13.2*
Grade 7	956	*7.3*	3,464	*19.4*
Senior Executive Officer	1,390	*6.4*	3,623	*15.0*
Higher Executive Officer	6,867	*14.0*	17,554	*22.3*
Executive Officer	36,788	*29.0*	54,650	*46.6*
Administrative Officer	108,111	*61.5*	117,728	*68.8*
Administrative Assistant	86,193	*79.2*	61,800	*70.4*
Other	22		270	
Total	240,919	*47.7*	260,236	*51.3*

Source: Equal Opportunities Division, Cabinet Office.

Note: Figures include those for equivalent grades such as professional and technical officers and scientific officers.

Women are increasingly represented at all management grades, although there are still relatively few at the most senior levels. Nevertheless, at the first management level—Executive Officer and equivalent grades—the proportion of women rose from 29 per cent in 1984 to 47 per cent in 1994. At the first level of senior management—grade 7—the proportion rose from 7 to 19 per cent. Women are well represented in administration, where they account for 62 per cent of staff, but less so in some specialist posts such as accountants, economists, scientists and engineers.

At grade 3 and above—the current senior open structure—nearly 10 per cent of posts were held by women in 1994, compared with 4 per cent in 1984. There are three women Permanent Secretaries and five agency chief executives (see pp. 15–16). The Civil Service has set a benchmark of 15 per cent for the proportion of top posts to be held by women by the year 2000.

Nearly 52 per cent of entrants in 1993–94 were women, although this is below earlier levels, reflecting a reduction in the proportion of women recruited to the lower grades. The progress report noted that women accounted for 99 per cent of new secretaries, but only 10 per cent of entrants to the professional and technical group. Among 'fast stream' entrants—assessed to have the potential to reach at least grade 5—the proportion of women increased from 25 per cent in 1983 to 38 per cent in 1993–94.

Career Development

Statistics for the Civil Service administration group indicate generally higher promotion rates for men, although the gap between the rates for men and women is narrowing and women's promotion rates to grade 7—a key management grade—are currently higher than for men. Promotion criteria are regularly reviewed to eliminate unfair barriers. Practices have changed in many departments involving, for example, the relaxation or removal of seniority requirements and attempting to ensure that promotion panels contain at least one woman—in some departments this is a requirement. Departments and agencies provide training and guidance for promotion board members on avoiding discrimination.

Women civil servants have received equal pay with their male colleagues in the same grade since 1961. Pay arrangements are now changing, with the extension of performance-related pay (based on annual staff reports) and the gradual delegation of arrangements for performance pay to departments; by April 1996 all departments will undertake their own pay bargaining. Monitoring of staff report markings and performance-related pay indicates virtually no variation between men and women.

Training and other measures to encourage women's development are being taken by individual departments. Several departments and agencies run the Springboard Women's Development Programme, which forms a personal and career development process, and stimulates the formation of support networks. The Civil Service College has developed women-only courses such as management development for women managers and fast stream development for women. Several departments also run their own women in management courses.

Flexible Working Arrangements

Flexible working patterns have become very extensive in the Civil Service, which generally assists equal opportunities and career development for women. Part-time working has increased considerably. In April 1994, 48,000 women and nearly 2,400 men were working part time in the Civil Service—18.4 and 0.9 per cent respectively. The proportion of women working part time has more than trebled since 1984. Part-time working is more common among the junior grades, but growing numbers of senior staff are working part time, including 13 per cent of women at grades 5 and 6.

Paid maternity leave was increased from 13 to 14 weeks in 1990 and a new entitlement of two days' paternity leave was introduced. Women with over a year's employment may take up to a year in total paid and unpaid leave. Additional career breaks have become widely available, being used mainly, but not exclusively, by women. A career break allows unpaid special leave for up to five years to staff with family responsibilities. Many departments and agencies operate 'keep in touch' schemes with staff on career breaks.

Homeworking arrangements are in operation in a few areas, and several pilot schemes are being tested. The Child Benefit Centre in Newcastle upon Tyne has a pilot telecommuting scheme under which 15 women staff are being provided with office equipment and are working both at home and at the office for a one-year period.

Childcare arrangements in the Civil Service have increased substantially. By April 1994 there were:

—46 Civil Service nurseries, 14 more than a year earlier;

—20 other nurseries operated as a partnership with other organisations;

—16 private nurseries where places were bought for civil servants; and

—121 holiday playschemes, compared with eight in 1987.

The Office of Public Service is encouraging the introduction of high-quality childcare facilities throughout the Civil Service.

Northern Ireland Civil Service

An action plan on the employment of women in the Northern Ireland Civil Service was published in December 1993. The main elements involve:

—the identification and removal of barriers to the progress of women into senior levels and specialist areas; and

—the provision of a framework within which individual departments and agencies can develop their own action programmes.

Other Public Sector

Measures to improve equal opportunities are also being under-taken in other public sector areas such as education, health (see p. 76) and the police service (see p. 98).

One area of public interest has been the armed forces where new areas of employment have been opened to women in recent years. Previously women were employed in a wide range of support tasks, such as administration, catering, communications, medical and nursing services, and legal services, but were excluded from combat roles. Women can now serve in combat roles in surface ships and as aircrew in all three Services—the Army, the Royal Navy and the Royal Air Force (RAF). The main areas from which they remain excluded are submarines, the Royal Marine Commando Forces, the Infantry, Royal Armoured Corps, Royal Artillery, Royal Engineers and the RAF Regiment.

There are 15 trained female pilots and 13 trained navigators in the Services, and more women are undergoing aircrew training. Over 1,800 women in the Royal Navy have served at sea in surface ships, and around 700 women currently serve aboard 25 ships. Service in submarines remains closed to women as the limited space available would not allow both men and women the necessary privacy, but this decision will be reconsidered in about four years, when the possibility of designing proper facilities for women in the next class of submarine will be considered.

The Sex Discrimination Act 1975 was amended from February 1995 to apply the EC Equal Treatment Directive to the armed forces, and Service personnel can now make complaints direct to industrial tribunals within the time limit of three months in the same way as civilians.

Table 12: Women in the British Regular Forces by Service

	April 1990		July 1995	
	Number	Per cent	Number	Per cent
Royal Navy/Royal Marines				
Officers	430	*4.2*	469	*5.4*
Other ranks	3,231	*6.1*	3,390	*8.1*
Total	3,661	*5.8*	3,859	*7.7*
Army				
Officers	1,230	*7.1*	1,097	*7.9*
Other ranks	5,816	*4.3*	5,347	*5.6*
Total	7,046	*4.6*	6,444	*5.9*
Royal Air Force				
Officers	1,136	*7.4*	998	*7.8*
Other ranks	5,625	*7.6*	5,079	*8.8*
Total	6,761	*7.5*	6,077	*8.7*
All Services				
Officers	2,796	*6.5*	2,564	*7.2*
Other ranks	14,672	*5.6*	13,816	*7.1*
Total	17,468	*5.7*	16,380	*7.1*

Source: Ministry of Defence.

Health and Social Welfare

Health Care

Since 1986 women's health has been specifically identified within the responsibilities of a minister at the Department of Health. The minister meets regularly with the Women's Health and Screening Delegation, representing 15 national women's organisations, to discuss women's health issues.

In addition to the general range of health services appropriate to both sexes, certain services within the National Health Service (NHS), such as cancer screening, meet the specific requirements of women. In 1987 Britain became the first EU country to launch a nationwide breast cancer screening programme, followed in 1988 by a comprehensive cervical cancer screening service (see pp. 72–3).

Life Expectancy

Life expectancy has increased for both women and men, although the lifespan of women still exceeds that of men. According to the latest estimates, the life expectancy at birth for women in 1992 was 79.0 years—up from 77.4 years in 1985 and 73.6 years in 1961— while that for men was 73.6 years.

The main causes of death are similar for men and women. Deaths caused by circulatory diseases, including heart attacks and strokes, represent nearly half of all deaths. Coronary heart disease accounted for 23 per cent of deaths of women and 29 per cent of men in 1992. Strokes were responsible for 15 per cent of deaths among women and 9 per cent among men. Deaths from lung cancer, at 4 per cent of deaths for women, were more significant among men, but deaths among women are increasing. Two causes of death of particular concern to women are breast and cervical cancer—responsible for 4.7 and 0.6 per cent respectively of deaths among women in Britain in 1992.

Health Strategy

The Government emphasises the importance of promoting health as well as treating illness. Preventive health services such as health education, and the responsibility that individuals have for their own health, play a major part in this. In 1992 the Government launched a White Paper, *The Health of the Nation* (see Further Reading), containing a strategy for improving health in England. Strategies have also been developed for Scotland, Wales and Northern Ireland taking account of the health variations in the different parts of Britain.[9] The long-term aim is to enable people to live longer, healthier lives. Targets are set for improvements in areas such as coronary heart disease and strokes, cancers, accidents and mental illness. A selection of the targets in England, including those of particular importance to women, is given below. Targets include:

—for coronary heart disease and stroke, to reduce death rates in those under 65 by at least 40 per cent by the year 2000 and to reduce the death rate for coronary heart disease in those aged 65–74 by at least 30 per cent—for stroke by at least 40 per cent—by 2000;

[9] For further information see *Social Welfare* (Aspects of Britain: HMSO, 1995).

—a reduction in smoking prevalence among adult women of at least 29 per cent by 2000, a reduction in deaths from lung cancer in women under 75 by at least 15 per cent by 2010, and a third of women smokers to stop smoking at the start of their pregnancy by 2000;

—to reduce the rate of deaths from breast cancer among women invited for screening by at least 25 per cent by 2000;

—to reduce the incidence of invasive cervical cancer by at least 20 per cent by 2000;

—to halt the increase in the incidence of skin cancer—which is more common among women—by 2005;

—to reduce the rate of conceptions among those under 16 by at least 50 per cent by 2000;

—to reduce the percentage of women aged 16–64 who are obese by a third by 2005; and

—to reduce the proportion of women aged 18 or over drinking more than the recommended sensible amounts by 2005 (see p. 74).

Health Education

Health education is promoted by the Health Education Authority in England and by equivalent bodies in Scotland, Wales and Northern Ireland. They advise the Government on health education, plan and implement health education programmes in co-operation with health authorities and other bodies, and sponsor research and education. The Government gives financial support to a range of women's health groups such as Breast Cancer Care and the Women's Nationwide Cancer Control Campaign.

A free booklet *Your Health—A Guide to Services for Women* (see Further Reading) gives information on family planning, maternity and other services, and includes advice on a healthy lifestyle and on common problems such as cystitis.

Maternity and Childbirth

Preventive services are available under the NHS to safeguard the health of expectant mothers and mothers with young children. These include free dental treatment, dried milk and vitamins; health education for parents before and after childbirth; and immunisation of children against certain infectious diseases.

Pregnant women receive regular care throughout pregnancy, either at a hospital antenatal clinic or from a general practitioner (GP) or community midwife. The birth may take place in a hospital maternity unit, a midwife/GP unit, or at home. Following the birth, the mother and baby are visited by a midwife until the baby is at least ten days old, up to a maximum of 28 days. Thereafter the services of a health visitor are available. Both the mother and baby also receive care from the GP.

The Government has given more emphasis to patient choice in maternity provision. In England an extensive policy review was completed in 1993 by the Expert Maternity Group. Its report *Changing Childbirth* (see Further Reading) stated that the mother and her baby should be at the centre of provision of maternity care, and that women should be active partners in decisions about their care during pregnancy and childbirth. *Changing Childbirth* was accepted by the Government in 1994, and the NHS is working to implement its recommendations over a five-year period.

Reviews of maternity care provision have also been undertaken in Scotland, Wales and Northern Ireland. As in England, the fundamental principle identified in these reviews has been the need for a service concentrating on the needs of the mother, and work to bring this about is in progress.

In 1994 a Maternity Services Charter was published. This sets out key rights and standards of service which women can expect to receive during pregnancy, birth and postnatal care, including:

— the right for a pregnant woman to choose where her baby is born;

— the right to choose who will be the lead professional providing her care—a midwife, obstetrician or GP; and

— the choice of whether to have a partner or other friend or relative with her during labour and birth, and who that will be.

Further standards for maternity services and care are set out in the Patient's Charter.

Human Fertilisation and Embryology

The birth of the world's first 'test-tube baby' occurred in Britain in 1978, using the technique of *in vitro* fertilisation. This opened up new horizons for helping with problems of infertility. The social, ethical and legal implications were examined by a committee of inquiry under Baroness Warnock. Reporting in 1984 (see Further Reading), the committee concluded that certain specialised forms of infertility treatment, including artificial insemination by donor and *in vitro* fertilisation, were ethically acceptable, but recommended that surrogate motherhood (where one woman bears a child for another) organised by commercial agencies should be prohibited. It also recommended a licensing authority to regulate infertility services and research. Legislation to ban commercial surrogacy agencies was passed in 1985.

The Human Fertilisation and Embryology Act 1990, one of the most comprehensive pieces of legislation on assisted reproduction and embryo research in the world, implements the report's main recommendations. The Human Fertilisation and Embryology Authority now licenses and controls centres providing certain infertility treatments, undertaking human embryo research or storing gametes or embryos.

Family Planning and Sexual Health

The Government's view is that decisions about fertility and child-bearing should be made by individuals, but that women and men should be provided with the information and means necessary to make their decisions effective. It regards family planning as an important health care service which contributes to maternal and child health and to the stability of family life.

NHS family planning services are therefore available to everyone, from family doctors and from health authority family planning clinics. Voluntary agencies complement NHS services. Family planning services are available to under-16s where parental consent has been granted, and exceptionally without parental consent if a doctor is satisfied as to the law and to Department of Health guidelines.

In England and Wales about 4.7 million women a year use family planning services. According to the General Household Survey (GHS) in 1993, about 70 per cent of women (or their partners) aged 16 to 49 in Great Britain were using a method of contraception. Oral contraceptives (the pill) were the most popular method, especially among the younger age groups. Sterilisation was used by similar numbers of women and men—5 per cent of women aged 20 to 34 and 22 per cent of women aged 35 to 49 had undergone sterilisation.

Britain has one of the highest levels of teenage pregnancies in Europe. Reducing the level is one of the targets in *The Health of the Nation* White Paper, and in 1991 there was a sharp fall in teenage pregnancies in England and Wales. Unmarried teenagers becoming pregnant are now much less likely to get married—in 1991, one in 11 pregnant unmarried teenagers had their baby inside marriage, compared with one in three in 1971.

Sex education is compulsory in all maintained secondary schools in England and Wales, under the Education Act 1993, although parents have the right to withdraw their children. Schools, parents, education authorities and health authorities are encouraged to work together to ensure that young people have the information necessary to enable them to take responsible decisions about their personal and sexual behaviour.

One area of continuing concern in sexual health is AIDS/HIV. Relatively few women have been infected by HIV, but the level of new infections reported is continuing to increase. By March 1995, 948 women had had AIDS, of whom 516 had died, and 3,391 cases of HIV infection had been identified among women. The Department of Health is undertaking a project on women's needs to examine how best to encourage access to health services; some NHS hospitals have set up family clinics for infected women or families with children. The Health Education Authority has developed a programme of activities for women to increase their perception about the risks of unprotected sexual intercourse. The programme includes a women's partnership project—with the Women's Health and Screening Delegation and the National AIDS Trust—to open up debate on issues related to women and HIV and to identify ways of taking action.

Abortion

Abortion is regulated by the Abortion Act 1967, which was amended in 1990 to introduce a time limit of 24 weeks for the majority of abortions. The Act allows the ending of pregnancy if two doctors consider that the risk of injury to the physical or mental health of the pregnant woman, or children of her family, would be greater if the pregnancy continued than if it were ended. An abortion on these grounds is allowed if the woman is not more than 24 weeks pregnant. An abortion may also be allowed, without a time limit, if two doctors consider that it is necessary to prevent grave permanent injury to the health of the woman; where there is a serious risk to life of the woman; or where there is substantial risk that the child would be seriously handicapped.

Abortions are carried out in NHS hospitals or in private premises approved for the purpose by the Department of Health. The number of abortions increased considerably during the 1970s and 1980s, but since 1991 the number has fallen. In 1993, about 170,000 abortions were carried out in Great Britain, of which nearly 65 per cent involved women aged 20 to 34. Two-thirds were performed on single women.

The Act does not apply in Northern Ireland.

Preventive Cancer Screening Services

Breast cancer is the leading cause of death from cancer in women over 35 in Western Europe. Nearly 16,000 women die from breast cancer in Britain each year. To help combat this, the Government has set up a national screening programme. All women aged 50–64 are invited for mammography (breast X-ray) every three years by computerised call and recall systems. Older women can request screening every three years. In 1992–93, over 1.6 million women were invited for screening, and 71 per cent took up the invitation. Of the women screened, 5.4 per cent were recalled for further investigation and 7.8 per 1,000 had a biopsy. The cancer detection rate was 5.7 per 1,000 women screened. Regular screening is expected to save many lives: in England and Wales an estimated 1,250 lives a year.

The first full round of the national screening programme for cervical cancer was completed in 1993. All district health authorities in England and Wales have computerised call and recall systems which enable all women aged 20–64 to be invited to have a smear test at least every five years. Similar arrangements apply in Scotland, where the age range is 20–60, and in Northern Ireland. Deaths from cervical cancer are declining; in England and Wales they fell from 1,903 in 1987 to 1,647 in 1992.

Most screening takes place in GPs' surgeries. Publicity campaigns and other initiatives are being taken to improve the numbers screened, especially in metropolitan areas where fewer people have attended both breast and cervical cancer screening.

Smoking

Cigarette smoking is the greatest preventable cause of illness and death in Britain, being associated with around 110,000 premature deaths a year. The incidence of smoking among women used to be much lower than among men, but the gap has narrowed and mortality from lung cancer among women has been rising. In 1992, 28 per cent of women and 29 per cent of men in Great Britain were cigarette smokers, compared with 41 and 52 per cent respectively in 1972. Also more girls than boys smoke. In England in 1993, 26 per cent of girls aged 15 were regular smokers, as against 19 per cent of boys.

In 1994 the Department of Health issued a strategy to reduce the prevalence of smoking and the consumption of tobacco by those unable to give up smoking. A three-year national programme of anti-smoking education, costing £13.5 million, was started in 1994 and is aimed at adult smokers, especially parents. Initiatives aimed at women have included campaigns targeted at young girls and pregnant women; smoking by pregnant women can cause low birth weight in infants.

Under the system of voluntary agreements between the Government and the tobacco industry, press and poster advertisements for cigarettes must carry one of the six health warnings which are legally required on cigarette packets. One of these draws attention to the danger of smoking during pregnancy. Advertising is prohibited in magazines where more than 25 per cent of the total adult readership are young women between 15 and 24.

Alcohol

The 1992 General Household Survey found that in Great Britain about 11 per cent of women were drinking more than the recommended level of 14 units a week.[10] *The Health of the Nation* White Paper set a target of reducing this proportion to 7 per cent in England by 2005. The Government believes that this requires a range of action by central and local government, voluntary and community bodies, the health professions and business. It places emphasis on policies to encourage those who wish to drink to do so within the recommended levels, and aims to promote healthier lifestyles and to ensure that help for people with drink problems is available at an early stage.

---

[10] One unit contains 8 grammes of ethanol. This is the amount found in half a pint of ordinary beer, a glass of wine or a pub measure of spirits.

Part of the funds of the Health Education Authority and its equivalent bodies is for alcohol-related health promotion activities. Treatment and rehabilitation within the NHS include in-patient and out-patient services in general and psychiatric hospitals and specialised treatment units, many of which are run by voluntary organisations. The development of services by local authorities to help people with drink problems and their families is being taken forward within the framework of community care.

The Government makes special funding available, both directly and through the voluntary organisation Alcohol Concern, to promote the development of local services by voluntary organisations, in accordance with the plans of the statutory authorities.

Drugs

In the six months ended March 1994 about a quarter of nearly 18,000 people with drug problems who went to drug services in Great Britain for the first time were women. Heroin was the most common drug used, and over half of the women were in their twenties. Mortality from drug dependence has increased in recent years.

The Government has made the fight against drug misuse a major priority. The White Paper *Tackling Drugs Together*,[11] launched in May 1995, sets out the Government's plans in the next three years to protect communities from drug-related crime, to reduce drug misuse among young people and to reduce the health risks and other damage related to drug misuse.

The Department of Health is encouraging the establishment of locally based services for drug misusers, providing a range of services from detoxification and counselling to rehabilitation. In 1993

[11] *Tackling Drugs Together: A Strategy for England 1995–1998.* HMSO, 1995, £7.

a directory of drug services for women was distributed to local authorities, health authorities and the voluntary sector. In 1995 a new national drugs helpline was started, offering free confidential advice and information.

The Government acknowledges the high rate of prescribing of tranquillisers to women, which can lead to dependence. There are a number of local advice and counselling services for women dependent on tranquillisers.

Female Medical Staff

The NHS employs more women than any other organisation in Britain. About three-quarters of NHS employees—who total almost 1 million—are women, including around 90 per cent of nurses and midwives. The Government is keen to increase the numbers of female medical staff, both in the interests of women who choose to make a career in this field and in recognition of the fact that it can be very important for some women, such as those from some ethnic minority communities, to have access to treatment by female medical staff.

The NHS is a member of Opportunity 2000 (see p. 54). Significant progress is being made towards meeting the targets for increasing women's participation in the NHS. Between March 1992 and September 1994, 38 per cent of appointments to the posts of chief executive/general manager were filled by women. Progress continues to be made on other targets, such as those for accountants and consultants, which have almost been achieved. A bursary scheme assists nurses and other professionals to train for management; 500 people are being sponsored to undertake management degrees. Significant investment in management and personal development has been made by the NHS, targeted at women in junior levels and at women from ethnic minority groups.

Social Security

Extensive changes have occurred in the last 25 years in the social security system. It has moved away from a system of protection for married women based largely on rights derived from their husbands' insurance contributions, to one where women are increasingly building up their own rights to contributory benefits and have gained access to most non-contributory benefits on the same terms as men.

Government priorities for women are the same as for men. The social security system operates under a legal framework which generally makes no distinction for gender. However, there are different patterns of use between women and men, reflecting variations in employment, earning levels, longer life expectancy for women and the greater likelihood that women will have caring responsibilities. Specific provisions within the benefit system take account of needs which are exclusive to, or more common among, women. These include the payment of child and family benefits to the mother in two-parent families.

Social security benefits provide financial support for people who have retired, are unemployed, are sick, are disabled, or look after sick or disabled people, while there is also help for less well-off families. Benefits are increased annually, the uprating being linked to rises in retail prices. The rates given are those effective from April 1995 to April 1996.

Mothers and Children

Maternity Benefits
Changes to the rules governing the two main maternity benefits—statutory maternity pay and maternity allowance, both payable for

a maximum of 18 weeks—were introduced for women expecting babies on or after 16 October 1994. One of the main changes was ending the requirement of two years' service with the same employer to be eligible for the higher rate of statutory maternity pay during the first six weeks. Now all those meeting the basic eligibility requirement—26 weeks of employment with the same employer—receive the higher rate.

Rates of statutory maternity pay and maternity allowance were also increased. Most pregnant working women receive statutory maternity pay directly from their employer. The current rate is:

—90 per cent of their average weekly earnings for the first six weeks; and

—the lower rate of £52.50 a week for the remaining 12 weeks.

Women who are not eligible for statutory maternity pay because, for example, they are self-employed, have recently changed jobs or given up their job, may qualify for a weekly maternity allowance from the Department of Social Security. It is payable for up to 18 weeks. Employees receive £52.50 a week and others £45.55.

Child and One Parent Benefits
Child benefit of £10.40 a week for the oldest qualifying child and £8.45 for each of the other children is the main social security benefit for families with children. Payment is normally made to the mother and is tax-free. The benefit is payable for children up to the age of 16 and for those up to 19 if they continue in full-time non-advanced education. In 1993–94 nearly 7 million families received child benefit in respect of 12.7 million children.

One parent benefit of £6.30 a week is payable in addition to child benefit to certain people bringing up one child or more on their own. In 1993–94 about 914,000 families, mostly headed by a woman, received one parent benefit.

Child Support Agency

An estimated 1.4 million lone parents, mainly women, bring up over 2 million children in Britain. The Child Support Act 1991 introduced a new system for the assessment of child maintenance with the intention of:

—ensuring that both parents meet their responsibility to support their children whenever they can afford to do so;

—producing fair and consistent results, and allowing for regular reviews to reflect changes in circumstances;

—reducing dependency on benefits by establishing realistic and regular maintenance payments; and

—retaining incentives for both parents to work.

The Child Support Agency was set up in April 1993 to replace gradually the court system for obtaining basic child maintenance. It is responsible for assessing, collecting and enforcing child maintenance payments and for tracing absent parents. Assessments are made using a formula which takes into account each parent's income and essential outgoings. It is expected that the number of lone parents on income support who will receive child maintenance payments will double in the long run.

In its first two years the Agency cleared over 900,000 cases, including over 450,000 maintenance assessments. Changes to the child support arrangements including the maintenance formula were introduced in February 1994 and April 1995 to take account of concerns raised by members of the public and MPs. Under the latter change, for example, no absent parent will normally be assessed to pay more than 30 per cent of net income in current child maintenance, or over 33 per cent for a combination of maintenance and arrears.

A White Paper setting out proposals for further changes to the scheme and improvements in the Agency's operation was published in January 1995 (see Further Reading). The Child Support Act 1995 amends the 1991 Act to implement the proposals to improve the provision for the assessment, collection and enforcement of child maintenance payments. They maintain the principle that parents, even if they live apart, should both support their children.

Income Support

Income support is payable to people who are not in work, or who work for fewer than 16 hours a week, and whose financial resources are below certain set levels. Groups identified as having extra expenses, such as families with children, lone parents, pensioners, long-term sick and disabled people, and those caring for them who qualify for the invalid care allowance, receive help towards meeting these extra costs.

Unemployment benefit is payable for up to a year in any one period of unemployment. The Government has announced proposals to introduce the Jobseeker's Allowance, a new benefit which will replace unemployment benefit and income support for unemployed people from October 1996. This would be more clearly focused on helping unemployed people into work.

‌‌

Family Credit

Family credit is payable to low-paid employed and self-employed working families with children, where one partner works at least 16 hours a week. Family credit is normally paid to the mother. The amount payable depends on a family's net income (excluding child benefit, one parent benefit and the first £15 of any maintenance payment) and the number and ages of the children in the family. Certain childcare charges of up to £40 a week can also be offset against earnings when family credit is calculated (see p. 87). A maximum award, consisting of an adult rate of £45.10 a week plus an age-related rate for each child, is payable if the family's net income does not exceed £73 a week. The rate is reduced by 70 pence for each pound by which net income exceeds this amount. From July 1995 an extra £10 a week is payable for people who work 30 hours or more a week.

Family credit is intended to help people who are bringing up children and to encourage them to stay in work. It also encourages those who are unemployed to find work, as it largely removes the likelihood of being worse off in work than out of work. Over 580,000 families receive the benefit.

Widows

Financial assistance to widows is available in a variety of forms. About 330,000 widows received widows' benefits in 1993–94.

Following the death of the husband, a widow under the age of 60, or over 60 and whose husband was not entitled to a state retirement pension when he died, receive a tax-free single payment of £1,000, provided that the husband had paid a minimum number of National Insurance contributions.

A widowed mother with a young family receives a widowed mother's weekly allowance of £58.85 with a further £9.85 for a child for whom the higher rate of child benefit is payable and £11.05 for each subsequent child.

A widow's basic pension of £58.85 a week is payable to a widow who is 55 years or over when her husband dies, or when her entitlement to widowed mother's allowance ends. A percentage of the full rate is payable to widows who are aged between 45 and 55 when their husbands die or when the entitlement to widowed mother's allowance ends. Entitlement to the widow's pension continues until the widow remarries or begins to draw retirement pension.

Where the husband's death was attributable to service in the armed forces, a war widow's pension may be payable instead of a widowed mother's allowance and at a higher rate.

Pensions

Average incomes of pensioners have improved, rising by 50 per cent between 1979 and 1992, although many more women than men have low incomes and are eligible for income support (see p. 80). The state pension remains the most significant component, but income from occupational pensions and from investments is becoming more important. About 85 per cent of pensioners receive income in addition to their state benefits.

State Retirement Pension

The state retirement pension remains the largest source of post-retirement income for women, but only around 25 per cent of women have entitlement to retire on a full basic state pension based on their own contributions on reaching state pension age, compared with about 86 per cent of men. The low rate partly reflects the arrangements in existence before 1977 under which married women who worked were given the choice of whether to pay full-rate contributions and receive a pension in their own right or to pay reduced contributions which did not count for any contributory benefit. In 1977, 64 per cent of women had elected to contribute at the reduced rate. Following the change in 1977, it is estimated that by 2010 the majority of women will have some pension entitlement in their own right.

The state retirement pension is payable to women at the age of 60 and to men at the age of 65. Over 10 million people—6.5 million women and 3.5 million men—received a state retirement pension in 1993–94. The Sex Discrimination Act 1986 (see p. 28) protects employees of different sexes in a particular occupation from being required to retire at different ages. This, however, has not affected the payment of state retirement pensions at different ages for men and women. The state pension scheme consists of a basic weekly pension of £58.85 for a single person and £94.10 for a married couple, together with an additional earnings-related pension.

Rights to basic pensions are safeguarded for people whose opportunity to work is limited because they are looking after children or caring for a sick or disabled person. Women contributors receive the same basic pension as men with the same earnings, provided that they have paid full-rate National Insurance contributions when working.

Occupational and Personal Pensions

The Government has encouraged the development of occupational and personal pensions so that both women and men are increasingly able to supplement the state retirement pension. About two-thirds of all pensioners now receive an occupational pension averaging over £70 a week. In 1993, 37 per cent of women had occupational pensions in their own right, compared with 19 per cent in 1979.

Occupational pension schemes cover about half the working population and have nearly 11 million members: 3.9 million women and 6.8 million men. As an alternative to employers' occupational schemes or the State Earnings Related Pension Scheme (SERPS), people are entitled to choose a personal pension available from a bank, insurance company or other financial institution. About 5.6 million people have contracted out of SERPS and taken out personal pension schemes.

Certain aspects of the 1986 EC directive, applying the principle of equal treatment to occupational schemes, have been incorporated into British law. The European Court of Justice ruled in 1990 that occupational pensions are pay and must therefore be equal for men and women in respect of service after 17 May 1990. Proposals on equal treatment in occupational pensions and on making personal pensions more flexible and attractive to a broader age range were contained in a White Paper published in June 1994 (see Further Reading).

Pensions Act 1995

The Pensions Act 1995 is based on two White Papers: that on occupational and personal pensions (see above) and *Equality in State Pension Age*. Provisions include:

—measures to increase security in occupational pensions;

—limited indexation of occupational and appropriate personal pensions;

—equal treatment for occupational pensions;

—equalisation of the state pension age;

—new arrangements for contracting-out of SERPS; and

—more flexible arrangements for buying annuities.

The equalisation of the state pension age for women and men at 65 would start from 2010 and be phased in over ten years. Women born before 6 April 1950 would not be affected; their pension age would remain at 60. The new pension age of 65 would apply to women born on or after 6 March 1955. Pension age for women born between these two dates would move up gradually from 60 to 65. Other changes in the Act affecting the state pension scheme which are aimed at improving the retirement incomes of pensioners include the full equalisation of treatment in state pensions for married couples, irrespective of whether the man or woman is the elder partner. Family credit would be treated as earnings for the purposes of calculating pension entitlement.

The split of pension rights at the time of divorce has been the subject of considerable public comment. At present courts in England and Wales can take pension rights into account but they are generally unable to order the division of these rights (see p. 32). The Pensions Act highlights the existing duty of the courts to take pensions into account in divorce settlements, and also to allow pension schemes to pay sums of maintenance to former spouses on the scheme member's behalf. A divorced wife would receive such a sum on her ex-husband's retirement.

Women as Carers

Women bear a large share of the responsibility of providing care, in particular for young children, and in caring for sick, elderly or disabled relatives.

Childcare

Day care facilities for children under five are supplied by local authorities, voluntary agencies and privately. In 1993, 985,000 day care places were available (see Table 13), 63 per cent more than in 1981. The increases have been concentrated in day nurseries (other than local authority nurseries) and in registered child minders, where the number has more than trebled since 1981. Around 90 per cent of those aged three or four attend some form of childcare provision.

Table 13: Day Care Places for Children under Five

Thousands

	1981	1986	1991	1992	1993
Local authority day nurseries	32	33	33	30	28
Local authority playgroups	5	5	3	5	3
Registered day nurseries	23	29	88	105	127
Registered playgroups	433	473	502	496	475
Registered childminders	110	157	273	297	352
Total	**603**	**698**	**899**	**932**	**985**

Source: *Social Trends.*

Note: Differences between totals and the sums of their component parts are due to rounding.

The Government recognises that family responsibilities can be a barrier to women returning to work and pursuing careers. It is taking steps to ensure further growth in the provision of day care. Government support of over £2 million a year helps voluntary organisations to develop new services, raise standards and train day care workers. Since 1983 the Government has provided funds locally to help set up day care schemes for school-age children. It has also encouraged school governing bodies to open up school premises for after-school care schemes. In 1990 the Government announced that the value of childcare facilities provided by employers would cease to be treated as employee income for income tax purposes.

In 1993 the Government launched a £45 million initiative to help expand the provision of out-of-school and holiday childcare places in Great Britain. The initiative, which is delivered through TECs and LECs, aims to:

—create up to 50,000 places over three years;

—help parents participate in the labour market by returning to work or training; and

—enable parents to extend their choice of work or working hours.

Between April 1993 and August 1995 some 40,450 new out-of-school childcare places were created. Consideration is being given to steps to encourage childcare provision in Northern Ireland.

To help people with family responsibilities who wish to work, families receiving family credit and other in-work benefits are now able to offset £40 a week of childcare costs against their earnings. This can be worth up to £28 a week in family credit. Eligible costs are those of registered child minders or nurseries. This is expected to help around 150,000 families and it is anticipated that 50,000 women will be able to take up work as a result of the change.

There has been a big increase in the provision of childcare under the Programme for Action to achieve equal opportunity for women in the Civil Service (see pp. 58 and 62). More private sector employers are recognising the benefits of out-of-school childcare. Some have opened nurseries and crèche facilities for employees' children, while others are helping through financial payments or by giving their employees 'childcare vouchers'. For example, the Midland Bank uses up to 120 nurseries (three of them belonging to the Bank) catering for over 1,000 children under five and it has set up about 40 holiday playschemes for its employees' schoolchildren. In 1993–94, 23 per cent of the members of Opportunity 2000 (see p. 54) offered places at workplace nurseries, as against 13 per cent in 1992–93.

Care of Elderly, Disabled and Infirm People

There are estimated to be approximately 4 million women and 3 million men in Britain who regularly provide some form of help or care for a friend or relative who is elderly, infirm or disabled, either in their home or elsewhere. Unpaid family carers are often women, typically wives, daughters or daughters-in-law of the person being cared for. About 13 per cent of carers are women aged over 65.

The Government fully recognises the role of carers. One of the key objectives of its community care reforms is to ensure that practical support for carers is a high priority. There has been a shift away from long-term hospital care to care in the community. Services for elderly people, for example, are designed to help them live at home wherever possible. These services may include help from social workers, domestic help, the provision of meals in the home, sitters-in, night attendants and laundry services as well as day centres and lunch clubs. Local authorities in Great Britain and health and social services boards in Northern Ireland are responsible for co-ordinating the assessment of people's social care needs.

Invalid care allowance, originally designed for men and single women, is a social security benefit of £35.25 a week for carers of working age who forego full-time work to care for a severely disabled person for at least 35 hours a week. In 1993–94, around

240,000 people were receiving the allowance, of whom over 75 per cent were women. Following a decision by the European Court of Justice, the Government extended the allowance to married and cohabiting women. Carers may earn up to £50 a week after deduction of allowable expenses without affecting entitlement.

Home Responsibilities Protection in the state pension scheme is designed to ensure that people whose family and caring responsibilities prevent them from working do not suffer reduced pensions in retirement as a result of lower contribution records.

Support Services for Women

Advice and help for women with problems is available through local authorities or from several voluntary organisations. There are many refuges for women, often with young children, whose home conditions become intolerable and who have nowhere else to go (see p. 93). Many authorities also contribute to the cost of support and counselling with families (such as marriage guidance) carried out by voluntary organisations.

Criminal Justice

In response to increasing public concern, the Government has toughened measures to deal with crime. Legislation has been strengthened through measures such as the Criminal Justice Act 1991 and the Criminal Justice and Public Order Act 1994.[12]

Violence Against Women

Women tend to be more worried about crime in general than are men, particularly about their safety on the streets. Table 14 shows statistics from the 1994 British Crime Survey. For women who feel vulnerable, the quality of their life may be affected, for example, by making them curtail activities such as going out to social events in the evening. When women do go out after dark, they often get someone to accompany them as a precaution against crime—in 1994 about a third of women said that they always did this, according to the British Crime Survey.

Statistics from the British Crime Survey for 1992 show that women are less likely than men to be victims of many forms of violent crime. Men are more likely to be victims of violence in the street, public houses and at work, with only 4 per cent of violence against men being domestic violence. Women are more likely to experience violence in the home, particularly from people with whom they live or have lived.

Over 90 per cent of domestic incidents against women are perpetrated by men, whereas only a quarter of domestic assaults

[12] For more information see *Criminal Justice* (Aspects of Britain: HMSO, 1995).

against men involve women. In England and Wales in 1992, 39 per cent of the victims of homicide were women and 45 per cent of female victims were killed by former spouses, cohabitees or lovers, compared with 8 per cent of male victims.

Table 14: Fear of Crime in England and Wales 1994

Per cent of those feeling very worried

	Females				Males
	16–29	30–59	Over 60	All over 16	All over 16
Theft of car	34	28	26	**29**	27
Theft from car	23	21	18	**23**	23
Burglary	33	29	29	**30**	22
Mugging	33	26	29	**29**	13
Rape	38	22	21	**25**	*a*

Source: Home Office—1994 British Crime Survey.

a Question not asked of men.

Sentences

There are tough penalties for the most violent and serious crimes. Life imprisonment is the maximum penalty for murder, attempted murder, manslaughter, rape or attempted rape and the most serious offences causing personal injury. The maximum penalty for indecent assault on a woman was increased to ten years in England and Wales in 1985 and Northern Ireland in 1989. The Criminal Justice Act 1991 gives courts in England and Wales powers to impose a longer sentence than would be justified by the seriousness of an offence on violent or sexual offenders who pose a serious risk of harm to the public.

In Scotland the High Court of Justiciary tries the most serious crimes and has exclusive jurisdiction in cases involving murder and rape. The maximum penalty for such cases tried in the High Court is life imprisonment.

Victim Support

There are about 370 victim support schemes—covering 98 per cent of the population in England and Wales—providing help and support to victims of crime. They are co-ordinated by a national organisation, Victim Support, which receives a government grant. Victim Support has about 10,000 volunteers, many of whom have special training to enable them to provide practical help and emotional support to victims of the most serious offences including rape. Similar schemes operate in Scotland and Northern Ireland. Victim Support Scotland, which receives a grant from The Scottish Office, co-ordinates the work of over 70 local victim support schemes. It has over 1,500 volunteers providing a service to about 40,000 victims a year. Blameless victims of violent crime in Great Britain may be eligible for compensation from the publicly funded Criminal Injuries Compensation Scheme.

The Safer Cities programme tackles crime and the fear of crime in inner city and urban areas through joint action by local government, business, the police and voluntary agencies. Twenty projects in England supported 3,600 crime prevention schemes between 1989 and 1995, of which over 300 were directed at women's safety, such as helping victims of domestic violence. This work is being continued in 32 new areas, including three in Wales. In Northern Ireland the Safer Towns programme has helped to establish domestic violence forums.

Government funding helps to support the Women's Aid Federation England and similar organisations in Wales, Scotland and Northern Ireland, which help to sustain women's refuges which provide a secure environment for women and children escaping a violent relationship. In 1993 there were an estimated 275 refuges in Great Britain for victims of domestic violence. The Government is also providing funding for a national telephone helpline for women.

Measures have been introduced to ensure that rape victims are not discouraged from reporting attacks. All police forces in Britain have clear policies on domestic violence, and many have specialist units. Rape examination suites have been set up by the police and staffed by women doctors and police officers wherever possible, and other action has also been taken with the aim of treating victims of rape sensitively. Improvements have been made in court procedure for those giving evidence. Victims of rape and other forms of sexual assault have the right of anonymity. Victim Support organises a witness service, with Home Office funding, providing support for victims and other witnesses attending Crown courts. About 40 witness schemes have been set up to help victims through the stress of giving evidence, and these will be extended to all 76 main Crown Court centres by the end of 1995.

Crime Prevention

Crime prevention advice plays an important part in helping people to reduce the risks of crime happening to them and in reducing the fear of crime. National publicity campaigns are a regular feature of the Government's programmes on crime prevention. The Home Office has recently revised its crime prevention handbook: *Your*

Practical Guide to Crime Prevention. This provides advice on practical measures which people can take to help keep themselves, their families and their property safe. It also attempts to demonstrate how men can play a part in helping women to feel safer.

In Scotland new crime prevention arrangements were set up in 1992, headed by the Scottish Crime Prevention Council and supported by The Scottish Office Crime Prevention Unit and the Police Liaison Group. An early decision was to shift the emphasis to crimes causing the greatest trauma to victims. This resulted in the launch of a video package on women's safety, *Seeing Sense,* including an associated booklet.

An interdepartmental working party on domestic violence, set up in 1994, is looking at ways of improving services to victims, encouraging local co-ordination and raising public awareness of domestic violence. A Ministerial Group on Domestic Violence has been established to decide how best to take forward work on this subject. A public campaign has begun to raise awareness of domestic violence, and includes posters and leaflets for victims.

Offenders

Under the Criminal Justice Act 1991, the Home Secretary is required to publish information to help those engaged in the administration of criminal justice to avoid discrimination on grounds of sex and race. The first such information was issued in 1992. In Scotland the Secretary of State is placed under a parallel obligation by the Criminal Justice (Scotland) Act 1995.

In general, women commit fewer crimes of all types than men, and a lower proportion of women offenders commit serious and violent crimes than do male offenders. By the age of 31, 7 per cent of women offenders will have had a conviction for a serious offence, compared with 33 per cent of male offenders. A higher proportion of women offenders commit theft than men; shoplifting accounts for 71 per cent of theft offences by women. In England and Wales in 1993, women offenders accounted for 12 per cent of those found guilty of indictable offences (the more serious offences) and 19 per cent of those found guilty of summary offences. For indictable offences, sentence or order was passed on 37,700 women, compared with 267,500 men. Over a third of women were granted a conditional discharge, compared with 19 per cent of men.

Women prisoners form only a small proportion of the population: 3.9 per cent of the prison population in England and Wales in April 1995. Only 13 of the 130 prison establishments in England and Wales hold women prisoners, who total about 2,000. Concern has been expressed about accessibility, and the Prison Service is considering a wider spread of women's establishments; this led to the opening of a new wing for women at Winchester prison in March 1995. Steps have been taken to ensure the maintenance of family contact, such as all-day visits and home leave.

In prison women are treated as a distinct group with different needs from male prisoners. Special attention is paid to specific groups, including women serving life sentences, mothers and babies and vulnerable offenders such as sex offenders. Mother and baby units in prisons are inspected regularly, and the number of places has been increased and standards raised. The Government's aim is to create as many opportunities as possible for mothers in prison to exercise and develop their parental responsibilities. The quality of medical advice and treatment has risen. Many women's prison establishments are currently served by male medical practitioners, but steps are being taken to encourage more female practitioners to apply for vacancies.

Prostitution

Under the Sexual Offences Act 1956, it is an offence in England and Wales for a man knowingly to live on the earnings of prostitution, and it is an offence for a woman to exercise control, direction or influence over a prostitute's movements by assisting or compelling her to engage in prostitution. It is also an offence to procure a woman to become a prostitute in any part of the world.

'Kerbcrawling' in England and Wales was made a specific offence by the Sexual Offences Act 1985. Thus, for the first time, male clients of female prostitutes became liable to prosecution in certain circumstances. The Government is keen to tighten the law on kerbcrawling by removing the present need to prove persistence, nuisance or annoyance by the kerbcrawler.

In Scotland offences relating to prostitution may be prosecuted under the relevant sections of the Civic Government (Scotland) Act 1982 and the Sexual Offences (Scotland) Act 1976. Kerbcrawling is prosecuted as the common law offence of breach of the peace.

Women in the Judiciary

Women play an important role in the administration of justice at the lower levels, comprising 47 per cent of lay magistrates in England and Wales in 1995. Women remain poorly represented in the judiciary (see Table 15), reflecting the relative lack of women within the legal profession with the appropriate seniority and experience. However, the proportion is growing and the Lord Chancellor has taken steps to encourage applications from women and to ensure that all who apply for judicial office are considered fairly. There has been an increase in the number of women judges and in recorders, particularly assistant recorders, which is one of the main entry levels to the judiciary. Between 1992 and 1994 the number of female assistant recorders rose by 22 per cent, and at the end of 1994, 16 per cent of assistant recorders were women. Recent changes to the judicial appointments procedure are designed to make it as effective and fair as possible. For example, specific competitions, which started in 1994 with circuit and district judge appointments, have been introduced to provide an appointments system open to all those who are qualified.

Table 15: Women in the Judiciary*a* in England and Wales

	1989		1994	
	Number	Per cent	Number	Per cent
Lords of Appeal in Ordinary	0	*0*	0	*0*
Lord Justices of Appeal	1	*4*	1	*4*
High Court judges	1	*1*	6	*6*
Circuit judges	17	*4*	29	*6*
District judges	7	*3*	29	*10*
Recorders	38	*6*	41	*5*
Assistant recorders	25	*5*	61	*16*

Source: Lord Chancellor's Department.

*a*Selected posts.

In Scotland the Lord Advocate follows similar policies as in England and Wales. The legal profession in Scotland is encouraging more women advocates and solicitors to make themselves available for judicial appointments.

Elsewhere in the legal profession more women are involved. The proportion of women called to the Bar rose from 28 per cent in

1980 to 43 per cent in 1993, when 676 women were called to the Bar. According to the Law Society, the number of women solicitors holding practising certificates more than trebled between 1983–84 and 1992–93 to 16,930, 28 per cent of solicitors.

Women in the Police Force

Women are also relatively under-represented in the police force, but the proportion of women police officers is increasing. In England and Wales the number of women police officers rose by 57 per cent between 1984 and 1994. At the end of 1994 there were 17,450 women police officers, 14 per cent of the regular police force. In Scotland women in the regular police force more than doubled in this period to 1,679 at the end of 1994, 12 per cent of the total. Women are now accounting for a higher proportion of applicants and recruits: 24 per cent of applicants and 29 per cent of recruits in England and Wales in 1993. Relatively few women are employed in the senior ranks, but the number has increased and the first woman chief constable was appointed in 1995 (for Lancashire).

Since 1992 all police forces in Great Britain have introduced equal opportunities policies and monitoring arrangements, while the majority provide equal opportunities training for officers of all ranks. All forces have designated an officer, mostly at assistant chief constable rank, with responsibility for equal opportunities issues.

Height and age requirements for police officers have been abolished. Flexible working arrangements are becoming more widespread. Following a pilot scheme on part-time working and job-sharing in six forces in England and Wales, this was extended to all forces from February 1994. Over 1,200 part-time posts have been approved. More than 200 officers, mostly women, took part in the pilot scheme, most of whom were police constables and many of whom were returning from maternity leave. Steps are being taken to introduce part-time working in Scottish police forces. The Home Office has inaugurated an annual award for equal opportunities in the police service and the winner in 1995 was Devon and Cornwall Constabulary.

In Northern Ireland a statement on equal opportunities was issued in 1990. An Equal Opportunity Unit in the Royal Ulster Constabulary provides advice and training to officers on best practice and monitors practices and procedures to ensure equality of opportunity.

Career Development

All recruits must satisfy standard entry requirements and undergo the same initial training. Women officers are deployed on the full range of police duties. Further specialised training is related to the duties on which the officer may be employed and, within individual police forces, women officers may receive specialised training in areas such as domestic violence, child abuse and sexual assault. Guidance has been issued to police forces in England and Wales on the principles and practice of a fair and effective career development and staff appraisal system.

Transport

Mobility

Personal mobility for women has increased with the growth in car ownership and in the number of women holding a driving licence. More men than women hold a driving licence, but the gap has narrowed. Between 1975–76 and 1991–93 the number of women holding driving licences in Great Britain doubled to 12.2 million. This represents 53 per cent of women aged 17 and over, compared with 81 per cent of men in this age group. In the age range 21–49 over two-thirds of women hold a driving licence, and over half of those between 50 and 59, but there are many fewer women drivers over 60.

Women are more likely than men to use public transport, accounting for around 60 per cent of public transport users; about 65 per cent of all bus journeys are made by women.

Access

When considering access to public transport, the Government takes particular account of the needs of women, including those travelling with children, shopping, in the advanced stages of pregnancy and the elderly. Through research and demonstration projects, the Government promotes the introduction of a wide range of features to make buses more accessible. Recommended design features are now incorporated in around 90 per cent of new buses. Similar design considerations are now being applied to railway rolling stock and to the vehicles being introduced on the new light rapid transit systems such as the South Yorkshire Supertram.

Safety

Concern has been expressed for women's safety in transport, particularly when using public transport, as a lone motorist and when walking in locations such as subways. The Government is working closely with public transport operators to produce a safer environment for all passengers, especially women. Measures have included the provision of better lighting and closed-circuit television at stations, subways and car parks, and safe transport schemes. It helped to sponsor *Travel Safely by Public Transport*, a passenger guidance leaflet produced by the Suzy Lamplugh Trust, a charitable organisation aimed at increasing personal safety and freedom from fear of attack.

On the railways new Networker trains have been introduced on several routes in the South East, permitting the withdrawal of the remaining single-compartment suburban rolling stock where passengers could not walk through the train. On the London Underground a programme of measures has been introduced and, accompanied by more police patrols, has led to falls in violent crime.

Measures to increase the safety of bus passengers and of bus staff have included installing two-way radios in more bus cabs, together with alarms, the use of video cameras and better lighting in bus stations.

The Government has worked closely with the Association of Chief Police Officers and the motoring organisations to produce advice for women drivers travelling alone to help them if their car breaks down. Motoring organisations have developed an in-car telephone for distress calls and give priority to lone women requiring assistance. More women are now using mobile telephones. Improvements in driver information and in motorway telephone systems are in progress. For example, in Wales a project is in progress to upgrade emergency telephones at over 100 locations and to provide 80 new installations. All the emergency phones will have advance signs, be clearly visible and be illuminated for use at night. Proposals to change the licensing arrangements for taxis and minicabs in England and Wales were announced in February 1995. Among the proposed changes is that minicabs in London would be subject to a form of control similar to that operating outside London, on grounds of public safety. There would be criminal record checks for drivers, and possibly a test to ensure that drivers have an adequate knowledge of local roads.

The Government is reviewing standards for the design and construction of subways in response to concerns about the safety of pedestrians.

The Media

Women are playing an increasingly important role in the mass media. A number have achieved senior positions in broadcasting organisations, such as Liz Forgan, managing director of BBC (British Broadcasting Corporation) Network Radio; Jenny Abramsky, controller of BBC Radio 5 Live; Andrea Wonfor, joint managing director of Granada Television; and June de Moller, managing director of Carlton Communications. Female programme presenters, newsreaders and radio and television reporters, such as Kate Adie, Moira Stuart, Sue MacGregor and Anna Ford, have become household names. A significant number of employees on newspapers and magazines are women, the greatest numbers working in magazine journalism. Women are found in reasonable numbers as columnists, departmental heads and editors, especially on magazines. In the media industries generally though senior management is mainly male.

Regulation of the media is the responsibility of the regulatory bodies, which have published codes including guidance on stereotyping, emphasising that coverage should take care to acknowledge the full range of roles performed by women.

Broadcasting

Existing broadcasting providers have adopted equal opportunities policies. Under the BBC's policy, nearly all its directorates have an equal opportunities officer and there are courses for women in management, film training and engineering training. The BBC also has a personal development programme for women. Under its workplace childcare programme, it provides seven workplace nurseries. There is an initiative to increase the representation of women in the BBC's workforce, and it has set targets of 40 per cent of women in middle and senior management by 1996. Over the past three years the BBC has made steady progress towards achieving these targets.

All the independent television (ITV) companies have an equal opportunities policy, and there is a joint ITV equal opportunities committee advising the companies and trade unions on good practice and policy. In December 1994 the highest proportions of women employed were in GMTV (56 per cent), which provides national breakfast television, and in Channel 4 (54 per cent).

The Government introduced the Broadcasting Act 1990 with the aim of making the regulatory framework more flexible and efficient, and giving viewers and listeners access to a wider range of services.[13] To ensure that equal opportunities are safeguarded and promoted, the Act places a duty on the two regulatory bodies—the Independent Television Commission (ITC) and the Radio Authority—to attach conditions to Channel 3, the proposed Channel 5, domestic satellite service licences and national commercial radio licences. These require the licensee to make arrangements for promoting equal opportunities in employment in areas such as training, promotion and conditions of service, and to monitor and review these arrangements.

Portrayal of Women on Screen

BBC programme guidelines include guidance on stereotyping and emphasise that programmes should take care to acknowledge the

[13] For further information see *Broadcasting* (Aspects of Britain: HMSO, 1993).

full range of women's roles. The BBC has taken initiatives to increase the representation on screen of women, ethnic minority groups and people with disabilities, and programmes aimed specifically at women are broadcast. For independent television the ITC lays down in its programme guide and licences the framework within which the ITV companies and Channel 4 must operate, and this includes guidance on the portrayal of women.

The Broadcasting Standards Council was set up by the Government in 1988 to act as a focus for public concern about the portrayal of sex and violence and about the standards of taste and decency. Its programme guidelines, which the broadcasters have a statutory responsibility to take into account, include sections on stereotyping, sexual humour and innuendo, and the portrayal of violence towards women in drama. It has also commissioned a number of research projects including some on women's issues. For example, in 1994 it published a study on the perspectives of women in television, which included an analysis of a week's coverage of terrestrial television, examining the frequency of women on screen and the types of roles played.

Pornography

The Government is committed to maintaining controls on obscene materials and ensuring that controls keep pace with technology. Several measures have tightened the law on pornography including:

—the Indecent Displays (Control) Act 1981, which prohibits the display of indecent material in a public place, or where it can be seen from a public place;

—legislation in 1982 to control sex shops;

—the Video Recordings Act 1984, which prohibits the supply of unclassified material in video form; and

—the extension of the Obscene Publications Act 1959, which now covers all forms of published material, including computer material and broadcast material covered by the Broadcasting Act 1990.

Further measures to tighten the law were contained in the Criminal Justice and Public Order Act 1994. These included a new police power of arrest in respect of obscenity and child pornography offences and additional search and seizure powers; an increase in the maximum penalty for child pornography offences; and an extension of the law to cover simulated child pornography on computer.

Advertising

Advertising in all non-broadcast media, such as newspapers, magazines and posters, is regulated by the Advertising Standards Authority (ASA). The basic principles of its Code of Advertising Practice is to ensure that advertisements are legal, decent, honest and truthful; are prepared with a sense of responsibility to the consumer and society; and conform to the principles of fair competition. Under the Code the ASA considers whether the portrayal of women in advertising is likely to offend the majority of readers or to cause serious offence to a minority.

Of the 9,659 complaints received by the ASA in 1994, 498 related to the portrayal of women, and 190 complaints were upheld. The ASA believes that advertisers are generally becoming more aware of public sensitivities towards images of women. It has reviewed the portrayal of women in advertising, most recently in 1990. It found that offence was most likely to be caused where women were portrayed in a way which exploited nudity or sex in a manner irrelevant to the product or service. Concern was expressed by a third of women and a fifth of men at stereotyping where women were depicted doing the majority of household chores.

In respect of broadcast media the ITC and the Radio Authority have both produced codes of advertising standards and practice which state, among other matters, that no advertisements may offend against good taste or decency, or be offensive to public feeling, or prejudice respect for human dignity. Advertisements must also comply with all the relevant aspects of British and EC legislation on discrimination, including the Race Relations Act 1975 and the Sex Discrimination Act 1986.

Sport

Women's participation in sport has risen, although it remains below that of men. In 1993, 72 per cent of men and 57 per cent of women in Great Britain had taken part in a sport or physical activity in the four weeks before interview in the General Household Survey (GHS) (see Table 16).

Table 16: Participation in Sport and Other Physical Activities in Great Britain 1993

Per cent participating in the four weeks before interview

	Women	Men
Ten most popular activities for women:		
Walking	37	45
Keep fit/yoga	17	6
Swimming	16	15
Cycling	7	14
Snooker/pool/billiards	5	21
Tenpin bowls/skittles	3	5
Darts	3	9
Weightlifting/training	3	9
Badminton	2	3
Running (jogging etc.)	2	7
At least one activity	57	72
At least one activity excluding walking	39	57

Source: *General Household Survey.*

A major effort was made in the 1980s to narrow the gap between men's and women's participation. This resulted in an increase of about 1 million in the number of women taking part in sport between 1987 and 1990, according to the GHS; participation levels in 1993 were similar to those in 1990. The numbers of women participating in 'physical contact' sports, such as football and rugby, have increased, and more women now play traditionally male-dominated sports, such as snooker and billiards. Sports and physical activities associated with fitness and healthy lifestyles are particularly favoured by women, with high rates of participation in swimming, keep fit and aerobics.

A number of sports have separate governing bodies for women, although the trend is towards amalgamation. However, competitive events are normally organised in separate divisions for men and women. One notable exception is equestrianism, where women riders compete on equal terms with men, often successfully. For example, in 1994 the British team of Charlotte Bathe, Karen Dixon, Kristina Gifford and Mary Thomson won the three-day event team title at the World Equestrian Games in The Hague, and Karen Dixon won a bronze medal in the individual event. Women jockeys have also enjoyed success in horse racing and point-to-points, while there are several women trainers competing on equal terms with men—in 1995 Jenny Pitman achieved her second win in the Grand National as a trainer. Mixed events in which men and women take part together are traditional in sports such as tennis, badminton and ice skating.

Netball is the main sport played predominantly by women. Other sports often played by girls at school include tennis, badminton, athletics, hockey, lacrosse, swimming and gymnastics.

Among the women who have achieved success at international level are Sally Gunnell (Olympic gold medallist and former world record holder in the 400 metres hurdles), Laura Davies (ranked as the world's top female golfer), Nicola Fairbrother (gold medallist in the lightweight category at the 1993 World Judo Championships), Sarah Hardcastle (winner of the 800 metres freestyle event at the World Short Course Swimming Championships in December 1995) and Alison Hargreaves (who in May 1995 became the first woman to climb Everest unaided, without additional oxygen and later achieved the same feat on K2 in August 1995, where she met her death on descending the mountain). England are the current world champions in women's rugby and cricket.

Encouraging Participation

In 1993 the Sports Council[14] produced a policy document on women and sport (see Further Reading). The aim of the policy is to increase the involvement of women in sport at all levels and in all roles. Six objectives were identified to support the policy:

—to encourage equality of opportunity for girls to acquire basic movement skills and to develop positive attitudes towards an active lifestyle;

—to increase opportunities and reduce constraints to enable all women to participate in sport;

—to raise opportunities and reduce constraints to enable women to improve their levels of performance and reach levels of excellence;

[14] There are currently four Sports Councils: the Sports Council, for general matters affecting Great Britain and English matters; and separate Councils for Wales, Scotland and Northern Ireland. On 1 January 1996 the Sports Council is due to be replaced by two new bodies: the United Kingdom Sports Council and the English Sports Council.

—to increase the number of women involved in the organisation of sport and encourage them to reach senior positions;

—to encourage organisations to adopt gender-equity policies and practices; and

—to improve communication about women and sport, and establish appropriate communication networks.

In order to assist the providers of sport in the implementation of the policy, the document included a series of 'frameworks for action'. These were designed to provide ideas for action that could be taken to develop opportunities for girls and women.

Leadership

During the 1990s the emphasis has switched from participation to encouraging women to adopt leadership roles, such as coaches, officials and administrators. Projects to promote coaching opportunities have been established by the Sports Councils in partnership with the National Coaching Foundation and the Women's Sports Foundation.

Women's Sports Foundation

The Women's Sports Foundation (WSF) was founded in 1984 by a group of women working in sport who were concerned about the lack of opportunities for women in sport and recreation. Its main aims are to represent the views of women involved in sport and to seek ways of improving their status. The Sports Council funds the WSF's National Development Officer to carry out project work on its behalf. This has included the establishment of women in sports networks throughout Britain and of career seminars for young girls, and the encouragement of sponsorship. In 1986 the WSF initiated the Sportswomen of the Year Awards and in 1992 it launched a nationwide awards scheme for girls and young women between the ages of 11 and 19. The scheme aims to encourage more young women to participate in sport and to pursue sporting careers.

Women's Organisations

There are hundreds of women's organisations in Britain covering the voluntary sector, political parties, religious groupings, trade unions, single-issue pressure groups and the professions. Some aim to improve the quality of life for women in the home by offering opportunities for social and cultural activities. Others seek to change the status of women in the political, economic, public, legal and social spheres. Certain organisations campaign on issues of particular importance to women, such as childcare, or represent the interests of a particular group of women, for example, teachers. Many have international interests and maintain links with similar bodies overseas.

Several organisations have many affiliates and act as umbrella groups for women's organisations. The largest are the National Council of Women of Great Britain (set up in 1895), with about 100 affiliates, and the National Alliance of Women's Organisations, formed in 1989, which has 220 affiliates.

Among the largest broad-based organisations for women are the National Federation of Women's Institutes, the Townswomen's Guild, the Mothers' Union and the Women's Royal Voluntary Service. These and many others are national in scope and have branches in all parts of Britain.

Founded in 1915, the National Federation of Women's Institutes has around 300,000 members. There are 8,750 Women's Institutes in 70 federations. Women's Institutes, offering educational and social activities, have traditionally been based in rural areas. Their activities include home economics, arts and crafts, sport and leisure pursuits, and campaigning on public affairs, educational and international interests.

The Townswomen's Guild was founded in 1928 and has about 100,000 members. It aims to advance the education of women, to encourage the principles of good citizenship, and to provide recreational and educational facilities to enable women to realise their potential.

The Mothers' Union, founded in 1876 and part of the Anglican Church, works to promote Christian family life through its departments for education, young families, social concern and overseas affairs, and through prayer groups. There are several other religious organisations such as the National Board of Catholic Women, the Church of Scotland Woman's Guild, the League of Jewish Women and the National Free Church Women's Council.

Organisations for younger people include the Girl Guides Association, founded in 1910 with the intention of enabling girls to mature into women able to realise their full potential in their careers, domestic and personal lives; and the Young Women's Christian Association of Great Britain, founded in 1855.

Women play a particularly active role in voluntary bodies. For example, the Women's Royal Voluntary Service (WRVS), founded in 1938, has 140,000 members (including 16,000 men). Its members carry out a variety of roles in the community such as assisting in the provision of welfare services to children and families, the elderly, the sick and vulnerable. Each year the WRVS delivers about 15 million meals on wheels (about half of those served in Britain) and a further 3 million meals in its lunch clubs. It receives a grant from the Home Office Voluntary Services Unit, which will amount to £6.2 million in 1995–96. Women also play an active role in other voluntary organisations, and are particularly concerned with areas of social welfare such as health and handicap.

Organisations representing the interests of specific groups include the National Association of Widows, the Carers' National Association, and Gingerbread (representing lone parents). The 300 Group, founded in 1980, aims to ensure that more women (at least 300) are elected to Parliament. It seeks to identify the special problems faced by women in entering politics and to support their efforts. The Fawcett Society, founded in 1866, strives for the acceptance of equal status for women in the home and in public life, and equal educational and job opportunities. It also runs the Fawcett Library, Britain's main library and archive on women's studies and the history of the women's movement.

The International Context

Britain has played a full part in formulating policies relating to the status of women in international forums such as the United Nations (UN), the European Union (EU), the Council of Europe, the Organisation for Economic Co-operation and Development, and the Commonwealth. It seeks wherever possible to implement the policies adopted by them.

European Union

Britain supports the steps taken by the EU[15] on equal opportunities. Under the Treaty of Rome, all member states have a duty to implement the principle that men and women should receive equal pay for equal work. EC directives have been adopted on equal pay (implemented in Britain by the Equal Pay Act 1970); and equal treatment in employment, vocational training and promotion and working conditions (implemented by the Sex Discrimination Acts 1975 and 1986 and the Employment Act 1989), and social security.

The EU has also adopted an action programme on equal opportunities for women. In 1991 Britain signed up to the third programme covering the period to 1995. The objectives include developing the legal framework for equal opportunities, and measures to promote the integration of women in the labour market and improve the status of women in society. Britain has also supported

---

[15] The European Union comprises the European Community (EC), the European Coal and Steel Community, Euratom and intergovernmental co-operation on a common foreign and security policy and in the field of justice and home affairs. Community legislation is adopted by the EC, not the EU.

EU measures on sexual harassment and childcare. In 1994 an EU White Paper *European Social Policy: A Way Forward for the Union* was published containing proposals on equal opportunities, such as codes of practice on equal pay, developing professional qualifications for women and publishing an annual equality report, starting in 1996. A proposal for the fourth action programme on equal opportunities, which would run from 1996 to 2000, was issued in 1995.

The European Social Fund, which aims to improve labour market opportunities throughout the EU by co-financing vocational training and job creation measures, provides support for women's projects.

United Nations

To mark the end of the United Nations Decade for Women (1976–85), a conference was held in Nairobi in 1985 which agreed the *Forward-looking Strategies for the Advancement of Women to the Year 2000*. The aim of this UN policy document is to achieve equal opportunities for women by 2000 through a number of broad strategies and practical proposals. Britain is fully committed to these aims.

In 1986 Britain ratified the UN Convention on the Elimination of All Forms of Discrimination against Women, adopted by the UN General Assembly in 1979. Signatories agree to take legislative and other steps to ban discrimination against women and to embody the principle of equality of men and women. This covers measures such as:

—providing for equal rights for women in political and public life;

—ensuring equal access for women in education and training;

—eliminating discrimination in employment and pay, health care and other aspects of economic, cultural and social life; and

—ensuring equal responsibility in family life.

Britain has supported efforts by international organisations to integrate women's issues into the 'mainstream' of other activities, so that women's interests are taken into account in all areas such as human rights and other social and economic issues. It played a leading role in the negotiation of the Vienna Programme of Action at the World Conference on Human Rights in 1993, which confirmed the UN's commitment to integrate women's rights into all its activities. Britain also supported the appointment in 1994 by the UN Commission on Human Rights of a Special Rapporteur to investigate violence against women. At the UN's International Conference on Population and Development, held in Cairo in September 1994, a 20-year action programme was adopted with a strong focus on women's reproductive health and action to improve the status of women.16

A report setting out Britain's progress since 1985 in moving towards the goals in the UN's policy document on the advancement of women was published in 1995 (see Further Reading).

Fourth World Conference on Women

The UN's Fourth World Conference on Women was held in Peking in September 1995 and attended by around 5,000 delegates from 181 countries. The conference reviewed the advancement of women in areas such as decision-making, human rights, education, employment, and health and social welfare. At the conference Britain sought action on human rights, improving the role and status of women in developing countries, and equality of opportunity in education, decision-making and working life.

The conference adopted a Platform for Action on a broad range of issues such as the family, rights concerning sexuality and

---

[16] For information see *Population* (Aspects of Britain: HMSO, 1995).

childbearing, inheritance rights and women in power. The Platform focuses on the need for strong national machinery for women; on improving women's representation in public and political life; on tackling violence; on the need for women to be economically independent; and on measuring women's unpaid work. Speaking after the conference, the Education and Employment Minister Cheryl Gillan said that the main achievement of the conference was in the endorsement of women's rights as human rights and the confirmation that equality for women was central to tackling other key issues successfully.

The Government is considering how to proceed on implementing the proposals in the Platform. Non-governmental organisations are being briefed and have been invited to submit their views by January 1996. Through the Cabinet Sub-committee for Women's Issues, ministers in government departments will be asked what they can do to implement the Platform.

Overseas Aid

The aim of Britain's overseas aid effort is to improve the quality of life and reduce poverty, suffering and deprivation in developing countries. In 1988 the Overseas Development Administration (ODA), which is responsible for Britain's overseas aid to developing countries, established a Women in Development Strategy. This stressed the importance of integrating women's concerns into all aid activities and emphasised that policies which targeted women in isolation would be unlikely to achieve the best results. Enhancement of the status of women is one of the key objectives of the overseas aid programme. In 1993–94, 12.7 per cent of the aid budget was spent on activities related to promoting the status of women.

Addresses

British Broadcasting Corporation, Broadcasting House, London W1A 1AA.

Cabinet Office, 70 Whitehall, London SW1A 2AS.

Department for Education and Employment, Sanctuary Buildings, Great Smith Street, Westminster, London SW1P 3BT.

Department of Health, Richmond House, 79 Whitehall, London SW1A 2NS.

Department of Social Security, Richmond House, 79 Whitehall, London SW1A 2NS.

Department of Transport, 2 Marsham Street, London SW1P 3EB.

Equal Opportunities Commission, Overseas House, Quay Street, Manchester M3 3HN.

Equal Opportunities Commission for Northern Ireland, Chamber of Commerce House, 22 Great Victoria Street, Belfast BT2 7BA.

Health Education Authority, Hamilton House, Mabledon Place, London WC1H 9TX.

Home Office, Queen Anne's Gate, London SW1H 9AT.

Independent Television Commission, 33 Foley Street, London W1P 7LB.

Lord Chancellor's Department, Trevelyan House, 30 Great Peter Street, London SW1P 2BY.

Northern Ireland Information Service, Stormont Castle, Belfast BT4 3ST.

Opportunity 2000, Business in the Community, 8 Stratton Street, London W1X 6AH.

The Scottish Office, St Andrew's House, Edinburgh EH1 3DG.

Sports Council, 16 Upper Woburn Place, London WC1H 0QP.

Welsh Office, Cathays Park, Cardiff CF1 3NQ.

Women's National Commission, Caxton House, Tothill Street, London SW1H 9NF.

Women's Organisations

Mothers' Union, Mary Sumner House, 24 Tufton Street, London SW1P 3RB.

National Alliance of Women's Organisations, 279–281 Whitechapel Road, London E1 1BY.

National Council of Women of Great Britain, 36 Danbury Street, Islington, London N1 8JU.

National Federation of Women's Institutes, 104 New Kings Road, London SW6 4LY.

Townswomen's Guild, Chamber of Commerce House, 75 Harborne Road, Edgbaston, Birmingham B15 3DA.

Women's Royal Voluntary Service, 234–244 Stockwell Road, London SW9 9SP.

Further Reading

£

| Changing Childbirth. Report of the Expert Maternity Group. | HMSO | 1993 | 18.50 |

Changing Childbirth. Report of the
Expert Maternity Group. HMSO 1993 18.50

*A Direct Line between Women and
Government: 25 Years of the
Women's National Commission.*
 Women's National Commission (WNC) 1994 Free

Equality in State Pension Age.
Cm 2420. HMSO 1993 6.50

*Equal Opportunities Commission
Annual Report.* EOC

*Equal Opportunities for Women in the
Civil Service: 10 Years Progress
Report 1984–1994.* Cabinet Office. HMSO 1995 11.95

Facts about Women in Scotland 1995. EOC 1995 Free

*Facts about Women in Wales/
Ffeithiau am Fenywod Yng Nghymru
1995.* EOC 1995 Free

*Fourth United Nations World
Conference on Women 4–15* Department
September 1995, Peking: Report for Education
of the UK Delegation. and Employment 1995 Free

The Health of the Nation: A Strategy for Health in England. Cm 1986.	HMSO	1992	13.60
Improving Child Support. Cm 2745.	HMSO	1995	7.35
Labour Market Structures and Prospects for Women.	EOC	1994	14.95
Looking to the Future: Mediation and the Ground for Divorce—The Government's Proposals. Cm 2799.	HMSO	1995	13.40
Maternity Rights: A Guide for Employers and Employees. Department of Employment and Department of Social Security		1994	Free
Opportunity 2000 Third Year Report. Business in the Community		1994	16.00
Report of the Committee of Inquiry into Human Fertilisation and Embryology [Warnock Report]. Cmnd 9314.	HMSO	1984	6.40
The Rising Tide: A Report on Women in Science, Engineering and Technology.	HMSO	1994	7.50
Security, Equality, Choice: the Future for Pensions. Cm 2594–I.	HMSO	1994	8.40
Cm 2594–II.	HMSO	1994	7.00
Social Focus on Women. Central Statistical Office.	HMSO	1995	25.00
Some Facts about Women 1995: Great Britain.	EOC	1995	Free

Stepping Out in Public—A Woman's Guide to Public Appointments	WNC	1994	Free
United Nations Convention on the Elimination of All Forms of Discrimination against Women. Third report of the United Kingdom of Great Britain and Northern Ireland. Department for Education and Employment		1995	Free
Women and Men in Britain 1995: The Lifecycle of Inequality.	EOC	1995	12.95
Women and Sport.	Sports Council	1993	Free
Women's National Commission Annual Report.	WNC		
Women in the Nineties: A Review of Past WNC Recommendations and a Strategy for the Future.	WNC	1995	Free
Women in Science, Engineering and Technology.	HMSO	1994	3.95
Women's Organisations in the United Kingdom 1994–95: A Directory.	WNC	1994	Free
Your Health—A Guide to Services for Women.	Department of Health	1993	Free

Index

Printed in the UK for HMSO.
Dd.301398, 2/96, C30, 566734, 5673, 339728.